THE APOCALYPTIC RESURRECTION OF JESUS

THE APOCALYPTIC RESURRECTION OF JESUS

ERNEST LEE STOFFEL

Smyth & Helwys Publishing, Inc.
6316 Peake Road
Macon, Georgia 31210-3960
1-800-747-3016

Printed in the United States of America.

Ernest Lee Stoffel

The paper used in this publication meets the minimum
requirements of American National Standard for Information
Sciences—Permanence of Paper for Printed Library Materials.
ANSI Z39.48–1984 (alk. paper)

Library of Congress Cataloging-in-Publication Data

Stoffel, Ernest Lee.
The apocalyptic resurrection of Jesus /
p. cm.
1. Jesus Christ—Resurrection—Biblical teaching.
2. Apocalyptic literature.
I. Title.
BT481.S84 1999
232.9'7—dc21 99-14805
CIP

ISBN 1-57312-261-0

To Betty
"As the heart remembers spring"
So will I remember you

CONTENTS

FOREWORD

Lee Stoffel brings a set of unusual gifts to the writing of this book. Every page reflects his gifts as a preacher, pastor, scholar, teacher, and writer.

Dr. Stoffel is a highly respected and experienced Presbyterian minister who has devoted most of his life to a preaching and pastoral ministry that has been influential far beyond the circles in which he has ministered. He has regularly faced questions about belief in the resurrection of Jesus from his fellow ministers and from members of his congregations. This book is steeped in that context, as ministers and laypeople will quickly discover.

In recent years the author has been engaged in a college teaching ministry in which the sharp minds of his young students have brought a further dimension to his reflections on the resurrection of Jesus. His pastoral and teaching ministries have sparked serious scholarly research into the first-century setting of the New Testament resurrection traditions. This distinctive study of the background in apocalyptic thought of many of those traditions is the result of wide reading and deep reflection.

As an experienced and able writer, Dr. Stoffel knows how to craft sentences and paragraphs that will hold the attention of his readers—something alll too few scholars can do!

It has been my privilege over several years to discuss the contents of this book with the author. On many occasions we discussed the New Testament resurrection traditions over meals in the heart of London. I treasure the times of rich scholarly and Christian fellowship we enjoyed together. We both frequently felt that some of the problems we grappled with are intractable, yet we never gave up. Resurrection faith is too precious for both of us to consider abandoning the quest.

I find myself regularly drawn to the comments of the eighteenth-century German scholar Bengel on the Gospels: they breath resurrection faith. This study also breathes resurrection faith. I commend it warmly.

—Graham Stanton
Lady Margaret's Professor of Divinity
University of Cambridge

PREFACE

The events of Palm Sunday are straightforward and direct. We believe we are reading something that happened. When we come to the resurrection of Jesus, the language and imagery suddenly change. Angels roll away stones. There are "two men dressed in white," a "young man in white," and an angel who speaks and one who does not. There are divergencies in the accounts of the Gospel writers concerning the appearances of Jesus. In Matthew there is an earthquake, tombs are opened, and the "saints" walk into the city.

Can we believe the resurrection of Jesus? It has been called a "myth" and a "legend." Some scholars, and more recently the Jesus Seminar, have called into question much of the authenticity of what Jesus said and did. Others speak of the resurrection as a "symbol." If the accounts of the resurrection are not to be dismissed as myths and legends, then how are they to be understood? Is there a credible witness in this language and imagery?

Clergy who think and read know the problem of presenting an honest witness. When it is time to deliver the Easter sermon, does the preacher step into the pulpit with the expectation of proving the resurrection beyond the shadow of a doubt? Or is proof of the resurrection covered by the loud voices of a large congregation singing "Christ the Lord Is Risen Today"?

There are also many thoughtful laypersons who are troubled about the concept of the resurrection. Those who wish to take everything in the Bible literally without question may not admit to a problem. But there are many believers or would-be believers who look for another place to stand in the face of the language used in the New Testament regarding the resurrection. Must these events be dismissed by the modern mind as unbelievable? If they are not to be dismissed and present serious difficulties in being taken literally, then what is this kind of language and imagery saying, and how can we understand it? Is there a positive witness here, especially in the Gospels and writings of Paul? Is there another place to stand?

Once an intelligent layperson, a young college professor, and a published poet, quietly asked me: "Can I believe in the resurrection as a metaphor?" Discussion of the resurrection as a metaphor aside, what I needed to hear and respond to was first the question, "Can I believe?"

Certainly it is important for Christians to hear about faith in the resurrection, but we also need to hear about that faith in terms that are believable and relevant. As seekers of truth, we require more than being assured on Easter that we are going to live forever. "Myth" and "legend" remain negative terms at best. How can either of these, or even the term "symbol," be made relevant in believing and preaching?

I am aware that once a subject such as the resurrection of Jesus is attempted, the stakes become very high. They become high for any preacher of the resurrection, and certainly for the Christian believer or would-be believer. My own belief in the resurrection of Jesus remains. A long time of study of the language of the resurrection, however, together with language used in other places in the New Testament, has changed the way I understand the New Testament witness to the resurrection and the meaning of Jesus.

In this book I point to one of the main strands that runs through the New Testament—a skein of apocalyptic language, imagery, and thought found in the Gospels, the writings of Paul, and the book of Revelation. I see this language as a distinct language that witnesses positively to the resurrection of Jesus and points to its meaning.

Let me say at the outset that I have not attempted to address scholars alone. I have attempted to base this book on sound scholarship and after much reading of the works of scholars. I have also tried to think of preachers of the resurrection and believers, or would-be believers, in the resurrection. For this reason, *The Apocalyptic Resurrection of Jesus* may be criticized as "falling between two stools." So be it. I am prepared for the criticism, if it proves to be helpful to preachers who must preach and believers who wish to believe that the New Testament witness to the resurrection of Jesus is more than myth or legend or symbol.

ACKNOWLEDGMENTS

In this study I acknowledge a great debt to my friend, Graham Stanton, formerly Professor of New Testament Studies, King's College, London, who now serves at Cambridge University as Lady Margaret's Professor of Divinity, a 500-year-old endowed chair named for the mother of Henry IV. He has pointed me toward valuable reading, and his suggestions and observations have been invaluable. All errors, of course, are my own.

Great encouragement and advice came from my friend Richard Ray, the editor of two of my books, a former editor at John Knox Press, and currently the Robert H. Meneilly Professor of Ministry and Church Leadership at Pittsburgh Theological Seminary. Without his constant encouragement, this book would not have been written. I am also appreciative of the encouragement of my colleagues at Queens College.

I dedicate this book to the host of ministers who preach the word of the resurrection and to "second-generation" believers and would-be believers who have neither seen the empty tomb nor sat in the upper room with the apostles, but "yet have come to believe." Consider me a fellow struggler in my efforts to believe and preach the resurrection of Jesus.

CHAPTER 1

A DISTINCT LANGUAGE FOR THE EASTER WITNESS

The Jerusalem where the first community of faith lived no longer exists. It was destroyed by the Roman ruler Titus in 70 CE. But at one time that community had known Jesus, followed him, and then finally deserted him in his dark hours. Peter, James, John, and the other apostles learned at his feet. There were also women who followed Jesus: Mary Magdalene, Joanna, the "other Mary" at the tomb, the sisters Mary and Martha, Jesus' mother, and others not named in the Gospels. In addition to those closest to Jesus, the Gospels suggest there were other disciples who were not part of the inner circle. After the death and resurrection of Jesus the apostles, female followers, and other disciples formed a community of faith. What happened to those people after the death of Jesus? What did they believe had transpired?

Something happened that accounts for the remarkable transformation of Jesus' followers and the burst of evangelical energy released in the first century. Unfortunately, the recorded voices of the first community or communities of faith are absent. Their witness became oral tradition, which has always been open to question. Some recent scholars have theorized that "Q," possibly a written source of the sayings of Jesus, was the original Gospel. Another group of scholars, the Jesus Seminar, questions the authenticity of much of what the

Gospel writers have recorded as Jesus' sayings and actions; they even question the resurrection.

The student of the resurrection of Jesus may view the event as having fragmented interpretations. Dealing with the New Testament as mainly myth and legend, however, so dilutes any "gospel," that it remains practically useless regarding faith. This is not to rule out New Testament study and scholarship concerning what Jesus said and did or what it is actually saying when subjected to historical study and exegesis.

The Apocalyptic Resurrection of Jesus does not deal with a fragmented authenticity, but rather with the New Testament witness as we now have it. Yet the question remains: If the New Testament, particularly the Gospels, the writings of Paul, and the book of Revelation, gives witness to the resurrection of Jesus, what form does that witness take? Furthermore, what are the implications of the form of that witness to understanding the resurrection both then and now? What are the implications for the preacher and for the person who is seeking a faith from the New Testament witness to the resurrection of Jesus?

The oral witness of the early believers, whom Luke calls "eyewitnesses and servants of the word" (1:2), would have become the basis of the Gospels after 70 CE and before 100 CE. They would have selected, edited, and compiled that which would serve their purposes. We have to depend upon them and others, such as Paul, for whatever witness we have concerning the resurrection of Jesus. But what is the form of that witness?

A Unique Language

Concerning the last week in the life of Jesus, the Gospel writers give us a rich variety of material. There are various encounters, incidents, and teachings of Jesus as he confronted his enemies or instructed his disciples. The events surrounding the arrest, trial, and crucifixion follow straightforward. The events of Palm Sunday are dramatic, and the pictures given appear to conform to the historicity of Palm Sunday. When we come to the resurrection, however, both the language and the manner of presentation change. All agree that the tomb was empty, but after that the accounts vary. For example, Mark gives no resurrection appearances, while the other Gospels do, and the accounts of those appearances vary from one Gospel to another.

Obvious in accounts of the resurrection are the different kinds of language and imagery used. For example, in Matthew an angel speaks to the women who have come to the tomb, announcing that Jesus has risen. There are earthquakes, graves being opened, and the dead walking in the streets of Jerusalem. Also in Matthew an angel rolls away the stone from the door of the tomb. In short, it appears that the language and imagery used to witness to the resurrection can be seen as a distinct language and unique form of remembering and witnessing.[1] This kind of language is found in the Gospels, the writings of Paul, and notably in the book of Revelation and is generally known as apocalyptic language.

The evidence of apocalyptic language is nothing new. It was known and used at the time of Jesus. However, paying more attention to this apocalyptic language and imagery when it occurs throws a special light on how the first community or communities may have understood and witnessed to the resurrection of Jesus. If the Gospel writers were reflecting the oral witness of the early community concerning the resurrection of Jesus, a strong part of that witness was either given to them in apocalyptic language and thought, or else they used apocalyptic language to interpret and reflect the witness they received. It was more probably given to them, since most Christian communities after 70 CE were not too enthusiastic about apocalyptic end-of-the-world imagery. More likely, the language was a part of the oral traditions they used, and what we have are tantalizing fragments of apocalyptic witness. If this is so, then the early communities of faith viewed the resurrection of Jesus in terms of apocalyptic thought, especially since they expected the imminent return of Jesus.

The words "apocalyptic" and "apocalypse" are often used to indicate something frightening, usually in connection with the end of the world. When something happens that is quite dramatic, bewildering, and generally terrible and catastrophic, it is called "apocalyptic." After the Gulf War I heard the burning oil wells in Kuwait described as "apocalyptic." At the beginning of that war an article in the London *Sunday Times* coined the phrase "apocochic," writing tongue-in-cheek about the end of the world being in style. Certainly most of what we hear about "apocalypse" and "apocalyptic" seems to dwell on catastrophes and the end of the world. The word "apocalypse" has become synonymous for catastrophe, or as my students often tell me, "the end of the world."

There is another side to apocalyptic language, however. It can be described as positive, triumphant, and comforting; and at the same time it is frequently poetic, dramatic, and highly symbolic. The word "apocalypse" comes from a Greek word meaning to "reveal" or "unveil." There is nothing frightening about the word itself. Apocalypticism has history, language, and thought forms all its own and was known and used at the time of Jesus and the apostles.

In addition to the Bible, there is a considerably large body of apocalyptic literature available to us, particularly in Jewish writings. These writings, called "apocalypses," vary in nature and cover a broad span of time. Nevertheless a discernible, basic faith may be found in them. In the Hebrew Scriptures of the Old Testament the books of Daniel, Ezekiel, Zechariah, and Isaiah are comprised of apocalypses of varying lengths. The one complete apocalypse in the New Testament, the book of Revelation, has its roots in Jewish apocalypticism.

All references to the resurrection are not apocalyptic. However, there is a definite skein of apocalyptic language and thought running throughout the New Testament, particularly in the Gospels and in the writings of Paul. Therefore, this different kind of language and imagery needs to be treated as such whenever it occurs, especially when it concerns the resurrection of Jesus or the meaning of Jesus' life. Angels rolling away stones need to be taken seriously. But how shall we understand this language and imagery? What light may it throw upon the early witness to the resurrection and the experiences of the first Easter communities?

Apocalyptic Thought and Faith

So what does this distinct language tell us? What does this seemingly bizarre language ask us to believe? Most apocalypses were written between 200 BCE and 100 CE. Parts of Joel, Ezekiel, Daniel, and Zechariah and the latter part of Isaiah were written during and after the Jewish exile in Babylon, after 586 BCE. In addition to the Old Testament, there are a number of other Jewish apocalypses written after 200 BCE that would have been known at the time of Jesus and beyond. These writings and this kind of language would have influenced the early witness to Jesus and the writings of the New Testament. How shall we understand this apocalyptic language in the New Testament?

Apocalypses in general see a battle going on between good and evil, between God's faithful people and their enemies. For this reason they seem to flourish in threatening times. When everything seems to be going against good, against God, and against people of faith, there is a need for reassurance and hope. Apocalyptic writers look at the world and the battle between good and evil and ask questions concerning human suffering and justice and God's faithfulness in the midst of the world's madness. We are not surprised that the Jews have dwelled on these questions, considering their suffering. The "short" apocalyptic answer is that God or good will win and that evil is doomed to destruction.

Since the Greek word "apocalypse" means "to reveal," this kind of writing and language should be understood as revelatory language. Apocalypses tend to reveal answers to the questions that plague people of faith with the assurance that God will win. This present evil or time of conflict and trouble will not rule. Those who hold on to their faith in God, even though persecuted by evil, will triumph. This victory can happen in time or beyond time, and sometimes in both, but it will happen. The judgment of God will occur upon evil, so the faithful are encouraged to endure until the judgment and victory occur.

Graham Stanton has observed that apocalyptic language poetically asserts that God will be victorious despite the oppression of God's people.[2] For this reason the book of Revelation has often been rediscovered through the centuries by people who are persistent in their faith. The book of Daniel originally spoke to the Jews struggling to keep their faith when their Greek persecutors had desecrated the Temple. It was later rediscovered by Christians in Nazi-occupied Europe during World War II.

It is no wonder that apocalyptic writing is difficult to read. The language and symbolism are bizarre. Number symbols are often used, along with grotesque animal and bird imagery. The sun is darkened, and the moon turns to blood. There are earthquakes and angels making announcements. We find God portrayed as sitting on a throne with angels all around. Angels are seen holding the four corners of the earth, and beasts are rising out of the sea to attack the people of God. There are horsemen with grim visages riding across the earth and even through time, for example, the famous four horsemen of Revelation. Angels are often employed as intermediaries or to make announcements concerning the purpose and work of God.

Sometimes the writers mystify us with their symbolism, and other times it is lost to us altogether. But usually the symbolism can be recognized as a special nonliteral type of imagery that can be understood when read as symbolic language. In addition, apocalyptic language can be cosmic in scope; that is, it may portray something occurring in heaven that corresponds to an event on earth. The event on earth takes place within time, but the event in heaven is timeless. This requires the reader to think both within time and beyond time—which is no mean feat!

In short, apocalyptic or revelatory writing was used to express truth when ordinary language was not sufficient. This means that we always have to look behind the apocalyptic expression and its symbolism to discover the truth that is being expressed. If we wish to interpret the parts of Scripture that use this language, we must translate the symbols and metaphors into our terms, which means looking behind the apocalyptic expression to discover its truth. For example, God sitting on a chair surrounded by angels is an expression of the truth of the sovereignty of God.

Readers of apocalypses such as the book of Revelation encounter catastrophes such as earthquakes, the moon turning to blood, and the sun darkening. These images have sometimes led readers to use the word "apocalyptic" to describe the end of the world or some terrible current happening. And when the catastrophes occur, such as the burning oil wells in Kuwait, they are called "apocalyptic." In apocalyptic writing, however, something else is meant. These dread symbols and others like them are used to convey the truth of the judgment of God upon evil, so terrible that it will be like the darkening of the sun or great earthquakes. They may not necessarily refer to the end of the world, but they refer to God's faithful people and to the destruction of the current enemies of God.

Sometimes a messianic deliverer is seen, and sometimes not. When he appears, this deliverer is victorious. Creation is renewed, and a new age is born. Death is destroyed. In Jewish apocalypses the victory of Israel is evidenced. In the book of Revelation the victory of Christ and his church is seen. All of this is accomplished by God, and people of faith are called to courage and patience.

The Origin of Apocalypticism

When we ask about the origin of apocalypticism, the answer is not easily given. In the Old Testament we first find it in Ezekiel, the prophet of the exile in Babylon. The latter part of Isaiah is also set in the exile. When we press back beyond them, we come upon Zoroastrianism, once a great religion that still has some adherents today. The founder is believed to be Zarathustra or Zoroaster. Zoroastrianism was the religion of Persia. Cyrus, the Persian conqueror of Babylon, is believed to have been an ardent Zoroastrian.

Zoroaster lived around 1000 BCE. He taught that there is one creator deity, Ahura Mazda, the "Lord of Light," with hosts of angels surrounding his throne. The world is made up of good and evil that contend with one another, but good or Ahura Mazda will win. Human beings are then called upon to follow the good in their lives as they participate in this struggle. Zoroaster also taught that the world will end with God's judgment and complete victory over evil. He believed in life after death. In his view, there was a final judgment, heaven, and a very horrible hell to which one would go if one did not follow the path of "light." The apocalyptic style of writing seems to have come out of these views, but it is doubtful that it can be attributed to Zoroaster.

In any event, it would appear that the Jews adopted some of these thought forms and the apocalyptic style of writing that accompanied them. At the same time they poured into them their own particular faith in God and in God's purposes. Even though they seem to have been influenced by Persian apocalypticism, they gave their writing a life of its own, according to their faith in and understanding of the God of Abraham and Moses. Most Jewish apocalypses were written after the return from exile. During these times they experienced the domination of various empires such as Babylon, Persia, Greece, and finally Rome. They were free for only a brief time during the Maccabean revolt in 168 BCE, only to be conquered once again and later occupied by Rome around 68 BCE. All these events, of course, had a profound effect on Jewish thought in regard to their faith in God.

The Jewish apocalypticists such as Ezekiel and Daniel promised victory over God's enemies and the restoration of Jerusalem. They took up where the prophets ended. Amos and Jeremiah preached the destruction of Israel because it had broken their covenant relationship with God. But when the apocalypticists took up the cause of faith following that destruction, they were dealing with the question: What about faith now? Can we still believe in God and God's purposes?

The prophet Ezekiel used a great deal of apocalyptic language. Imagine living in Babylon after the destruction of Jerusalem and the Temple in 586 BCE. Ezekiel lived through it all, including the times before and after the destruction. He was deported with the other captives and placed in a concentration camp in Babylon. There he became a prophet and pastor to the exiles who had lost hope.

Jerusalem was in ruins. The Jewish homeland was no more. The promises to Abraham seemed lost, to say nothing of hopes for a deliverer such as David. In that atmosphere of hopelessness, Ezekiel became the prophet of hope. He promised the return to Jerusalem and the restoration of the city and Temple. He preached the future victory of God and God's people and urged his people to hold on to their faith. The most famous vision of this restoration is found in Ezekiel 37, where the valley of dry bones (Israel) is restored to life: "Then he said to me, 'Mortal, these bones are the whole house of Israel. . . . I am going to open your graves . . . and bring you back to the land of Israel' " (vv. 11, 12).

Ezekiel 1 is a bizarre and highly symbolic picture of the sovereign God upon the throne. There are four creatures beneath the throne who are symbolic of all creation. The message of this apocalyptic picture is that God is sovereign over all things and will triumph over Israel's enemies. In other words, Ezekiel sees the nation "resurrected."

In keeping with apocalyptic imagery, the picture is dramatic and intended to convey a message of hope and encouragement. It promises the defeat of the evil holding Jewish hopes hostage. It promises restoration. It urges faith, even when the forces of evil give every appearance of domination. The sovereignty of God and the promise of God's faithfulness are declared. God's purposes will be carried out, and Ezekiel urges his dispirited fellow exiles to trust in God's faithfulness, despite all evidence to the contrary. "I will bring you back . . . and you shall know that I am the Lord" (vv. 12, 13).

Ezekiel remains in the stream of the great prophets of the past such as Amos and Jeremiah. He believes in Israel's covenant responsibility with God. His main purpose is to preach that God has not abandoned them, even though they have suffered the calamity of judgment promised by Jeremiah and the other prophets.

It is true that Ezekiel lacks the great emphasis of Amos on social justice. The apocalyptic writers have been criticized because of their neglect of social issues. Some have suggested that they see nothing people of faith can do except wait and hope. But in fairness, social justice is not Ezekiel's main concern. His main purpose is to rekindle faith in the God of Israel, who is seen as the one sovereign Creator.

Like Ezekiel, Daniel is set in Babylon with the exiles. However, the book was actually written at a much later period, possibly during the Maccabean period (168 BCE) when the Jews had returned and rebuilt Jerusalem and the Temple. Nevertheless, upon their return they knew no real freedom. They continued under the Persian thumb after they conquered their original captors, the Babylonians. Alexander the Great then conquered the Persians. Following the death of Alexander, Greek generals and their successors ruled various parts of the former Persian empire, including Palestine. Greek rule was very repressive, particularly of the Jewish religion. In 168 BCE the Maccabee brothers led a revolt. For a brief moment they were free, but independence was lost a few short years later. Again the age-old question arises: Is God faithful? What is the use of faith?

The first part of the book of Daniel is the familiar story of Daniel being thrown into the lions' den for holding to his faith in the Lord, the God of Israel. His deliverance by the Lord encouraged those who would be tempted to abandon their faith. The second part of the book, chapters 7–12, is written in apocalyptic style. Four beasts rise out of the sea, symbolizing four kingdoms that had oppressed the Jews: Babylon, Media, Persia, and Greece. There is a vision of the throne of God: "An Ancient One took his throne, his clothing was white as snow" (7:9). "To him was given dominion and glory and kingship . . . an everlasting dominion that shall not pass away" (v. 14). Scholars differ as to the identity of this person. It may be seen as symbolic of the victory of the faithful in Israel or as an individual messiah who is triumphant, more probably the latter.[3] The message is that the one on the throne is greater than the kingdoms that oppress Israel. Just as Daniel held on to his faith, so the people of God are encouraged to remain faithful and believe in their eventual victory through the one on the throne.

Connected with this encouraging picture is a promise in Daniel 12:2. "Many of those who sleep in the dust of the earth shall awake, some to everlasting life, and some to shame and everlasting contempt." This prediction is reminiscent of the Zoroastrian concept of final judgment. More importantly, it is the first mention of a general resurrection in the Hebrew Scriptures. Although the idea of the renewal of life appears in many ancient settings, especially with Zoroaster and the Persian religion, the promise here has a special significance. Here the author of Daniel promises a resurrection of God's faithful people and the triumph of God over their enemies. This image goes beyond Ezekiel's vision of a resurrected nation. No more than this is said, and no time table is given. This belief in a resurrection will persist to the time of Jesus. It is important because it affirms God's faithfulness, even beyond death. It adds an element to apocalyptic thought that is beyond time.

Zechariah 1–9 is also set primarily in Babylon during the exile. Apocalyptic imagery and language abound: four horsemen, four winds, four horns, Satan as the accuser, and a flying scroll. The author writes during the return of a group of exiles led by Joshua, the high priest and Zerubbabel (3:6; 6:11). The triumph of the Lord is announced: "Jerusalem shall be inhabited as villages without walls. . . . For I will be a wall of fire all around it, says the Lord, and I will be the glory within it" (2:4-5). A Christian hymn has taken notice of the language and imagery used here to announce God's victory. The symbolism here is much larger than a literal reference to the rebuilding of the walls and city of Jerusalem by the returning exiles. A greater victory and restoration are announced. The Christian hymn, "Glorious Things of You Are Spoken," sees this victory in Christ's Church:

> Glorious things of you are spoken,
> Zion, city of our God;
> He whose word cannot be broken
> Formed you for his own abode.
>
> On the Rock of Ages founded,
> What can shake your sure repose?
> With salvation's walls surrounded,
> You may smile at all your foes.
>
> —John Newton, 1779; alt. 1972

This apocalyptic imagery is rich with a cosmic faith that is able to span time and reach beyond time. It has been part and parcel of both Jewish and Christian faith. The imagery is "beggared," when taken literally, but glows with a great light when its symbolism is allowed to speak. Christian preachers have taken this text to speak of the security of the church.

Zechariah 9–14 is set in another time, when Greece was the dominant power in Palestine. Although the imagery is not as colorful as in chapters 1-9, the message remains the same. There will come a day of the Lord, and it will mean new life for Israel (9:1-11:17). The day of the Lord for the pre-exilic prophets such as Amos was a time of darkness when Israel would be judged for breaking the covenant. Here the day of the Lord is a victorious day. The Jews will be gathered from among the nations. Egypt and Assyria are mentioned as representative of the nations that have oppressed them. Their destruction is assured.

To take this literally is to miss the broader concept of God's victory over evil. To see this promise fulfilled in the present state of Israel, or even to expect its fulfillment in some future state of Israel, is to miss the greater faith here. The "walls" of God that are to surround Jerusalem are broader than the measure of man's mind. The victory of God implied by the rich apocalyptic imagery of Ezekiel, Daniel, and Zechariah reaches into the New Testament, to the exaltation of Jesus and the New Israel that Christians see in the church.

Approaching the New Testament

As we approach the New Testament, one Jewish apocalypse outside the Old Testament should particularly be noted. Dated between 200 BCE and the beginning of the first century, 1 Enoch is quoted in the New Testament book Jude, verses 14–15. According to James H. Charlesworth, "Few other apocryphal books so indelibly marked the religious history and thought of the time of Jesus."[4] The writer was concerned with what was happening to the Jewish people, first under the Babylonians and Greeks and soon Rome. Is God still faithful? Are the wicked to triumph and the righteous to fail?

So in 1 Enoch there is particular stress on the coming judgment of the wicked and the vindication of the righteous. There is also the concept of the messiah, sometimes called the

Righteous One or the Elect One who will be exalted as the deliverer of Israel. The Danielic theme of the resurrection of the righteous is also found in 1 Enoch, together with a throne of judgment and the concept of the New Jerusalem. There is one called the "Antecedent of Time" who is reminiscent of Daniel's Ancient One. The Antecedent of Time is seen sitting on the throne of his glory, with the books of the living ones open before him (47:31). Enoch looks forward to a "day" when heaven and earth will be transformed. It suggests the knowledge and use of apocalyptic language and imagery at the time of Jesus and also carries Daniel's concept of the resurrection of the just to the time of Jesus.

The Jews had various views of the resurrection. The Sadducees did not believe in a resurrection (Mark 12:18). The Pharisees believed in a resurrection, but viewed it as a permanent raising still in the future and possibly as more like Daniel's idea of the resurrection of the just. If a person was restored from death, it was only a temporary restoration; they would die again, as in the case of Lazarus. There was also the view that a person restored from death was only a ghost, as in the Witch of Endor raising the ghost of Samuel (1 Sam 28). A Jew had to see continuity between a body laid in a tomb and a person known to be alive afterward.

Apparently, the writings from Ezekiel to the time of Jesus reaches forward in faith that the God of Abraham can be trusted. Faith and righteousness will be vindicated. The despoilers of the earth will not inherit, and there is a judgment waiting for evil. Even though justice might not prevail in this life, there is lifted up a hope for resurrection and vindication beyond this life. But as the author of Hebrews in the New Testament wrote, "All of these died in faith without having received the promises, but from a distance they saw and greeted them" (11:13). Faith remained that God could be trusted.

In the New Testament, apocalyptic language appears sufficiently to call for our attention, particularly that linked with the resurrection of Jesus.[5] In this language the resurrection is not just the exaltation of a good man or even the promise of eternal life. Rather, it is something that calls for an even larger faith in God: Does evil have the last word? Do God and goodness matter in the world with its wars, famines, disease, and pain? Is there a power and love that is larger than all these, and will that power and love win? In the New Testament the death and resurrection of Jesus take their places squarely within these questions.

We turn now to the New Testament witness of Jesus and his resurrection. Our principal sources are the writings of Paul; the Gospels of Mark, Matthew, Luke, and John; and the book of Revelation. Each has the resurrection as the centerpiece of its witness. As Paul witnesses, and as each evangelist tells the story of Jesus, the underlying affirmation from the beginning is the faithfulness of God in exalting Jesus. In this sense, all are in the true apocalyptic tradition. Their witness to the resurrection and to Jesus himself takes on new power when read in the light of that tradition. This is especially true wherever their witness takes on the colors of apocalyptic language and thought.

Notes

[1]Pheme Perkins," *Resurrection, New Testament Witness, and Contemporary Reflection* (Garden City NY: Doubleday & Co., 1984), uses the phrase "a distinct language for the resurrection" and writes of apocalyptic language as "the language of resurrection." From where did these apocalyptic themes arise if not from Jewish apocalypses? In connection with his discussion of the resurrection, Schillebeecx, *Jesus, An Experiment in Christology* (London: Collins-St. James Place, 1979), wrote of "exaltation language" in the early church. According to Klaus Koch, *The Recovery of Apocalyptic* (Naperville IL: Alec R. Allenson, 1970), "the apocalyptic world of ideas . . . permitted a part of late Israel to merge into early Christianity." Perkins believes "one finds Christians combining the apocalyptic code of divine victory at the parousia with the belief that the victory over death has been accomplished." Perkins also expresses a need to "recover a way into the reality of that early world of discourse."

[2]Graham Stanton, *Gospel Truth? New Light on Jesus and the Gospels* (London: HarperCollins, 1995).

[3]I am aware of the question concerning whether or not Jesus saw himself as the coming victorious Son of Man. Certainly his quoted references to the coming Son of Man carried with them the note of triumph. His comments are veiled in regard to whether he was speaking of himself or of the future triumph of God. This also has to do with the question of whether or not Jesus was an apocalypticist. In the Gospels he speaks apocalyptically at times in the sense that he believed in the coming triumph of the kingdom-rule of God. His part in that triumph is veiled.

[4]See James H. Charlesworth, ed., *The Old Testament Pseudepigrapha*, vol. 1 (Garden City NY: Doubleday & Co., 1985) 8.

[5]In regard to the early community as an apocalyptic community and quite possibly using apocalyptic language to refer to the resurrection of Jesus, Ernst Käsemann's *New Testament Questions of Today* (London: SCM, 1969) is relevant. Reference is made particularly to chapter 5, "On the Subject of Primitive Christian Apocalyptic." Käsemann rightly challenges us to find a specific term "for the particular form of eschatology that attempts to talk about ultimate history." Apocalyptic, I believe, is the only term that will fit. Since the resurrection of Jesus has to do with ultimate history, it should be considered in apocalyptic terms.

CHAPTER 2

PAUL'S WITNESS

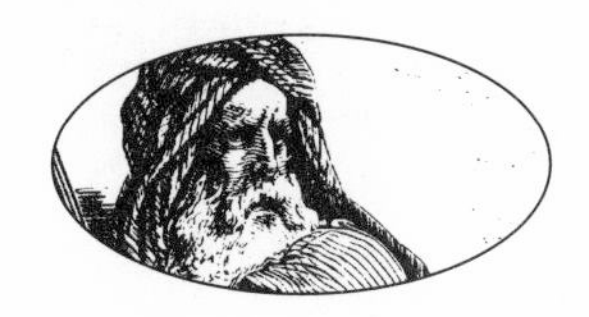

Paul's witness to the resurrection of Jesus is the earliest account we have prior to the Gospels. His theological reflections upon the Christian faith are unparalleled, but when he speaks of the resurrection of Jesus, it is in the context of that which he has "received" (1 Cor 11:23).

In his letter to the Galatian church, Paul writes of three years he spent in Arabia after his conversion. Following those years of reflection, he went to Jerusalem to visit Peter for fifteen days. He saw none of the other apostles except James, the brother of Jesus. We can speculate that those conversations brought him further information on what Jesus said and did and about the faith of the Jerusalem community. After his visit to Jerusalem, Paul went to Syria and Cilicia (Gal 1:21). Fourteen years passed before he visited Jerusalem again, where he was still unknown "by sight" to the churches of Judea (v. 22). This means that some seventeen years passed after his conversion before he became visible to the early communities of faith. But when Paul wrote his letters, they were surely known to early believers, even though his physical features were not. There is no evidence that his witness was contradicted.

What was happening to the communities of faith during this time? We must assume that Christian witnesses were active in other places. The oral gospel was developing, and perhaps some written material, but of that we cannot be certain. A body of faith would be developed together with a defined witness concerning the events of Jesus' last week. We can believe that Paul would have been knowledgeable of their early witness.

As far as Jerusalem was concerned, he kept a low profile, although Peter and James knew him. His previous reputation as a persecutor of the church remained with him. According to Luke in Acts 11:25, Barnabas went to Tarsus to look for Paul and to take him to Antioch in Syria as a co-pastor. This would mean that his reputation with the leaders at Jerusalem was positive, at least with such an influential leader as Barnabas. His apostolic claim, however, may not have been recognized.

Paul's missionary journeys are a firm part of the tradition of the later church and perhaps of the early church. Sometime in the latter part of the first century the church at Antioch in Syria sent Paul and Barnabas as the first missionaries. They preached the good news of the crucified and risen Jesus as the Messiah.

When Paul wrote of the resurrection of Jesus, he assumed the resurrection took place, but two omissions stand out: He made no reference to the appearances to the women as they are found in Matthew and Luke, and he said nothing about the empty tomb. In Galatians 1:15-16 Paul notes that God set him apart before he was born and called him through grace. "God . . . was pleased to reveal his Son to me, so that I might proclaim him among the Gentiles."

Paul does not elaborate on his experience on the Damascus Road, although he was dealing with his apostolic authority, a very serious matter. Later, in his letter to the Roman church, he would write of Jesus as having been "declared to be Son of God in power according to the spirit of holiness by resurrection from the dead" (Rom 1:4). Clearly the foundation of his faith was that God had raised Jesus, but he saw no need to go into details.

"The Lord . . . Will Descend" (1 Thess 4:16)

Paul's earliest texts and the earliest recorded parts of the New Testament do not deal with the resurrection but with the second coming of Jesus and the endtimes. In his first letter to the church at Thessalonica, Paul simply recites the faith: "We believe that Jesus died and rose again" (4:14). He puts his main emphasis on the endtimes and the return of Jesus. What he says concerning the endtimes is familiar to Christians, since part of it is sometimes read at Christian funerals (4:13-18). Paul comforts the Christians at Thessalonica who have lost loved ones. He says Jesus will bring them with him when he returns. What we have here is perhaps the earliest Christian expectation of the endtimes and an indication that Paul expected the imminent return of Jesus. The early Christians, including Paul, expected Jesus to return from heaven in their lifetime. They assumed Jesus was in heaven, but as time went on and Jesus did not return, they had to readjust their thinking. Paul assumes that Jesus is exalted in heaven and will return, even though the return is delayed.

Paul uses apocalyptic language and imagery to speak of Christ's return. The Lord, "with a cry of command, with the archangel's call and with the sound of God's trumpet, will descend from heaven" (4:16). The language is triumphant, colored by the archangel and the trumpet of God. This is the language of Daniel 12:2, which looks for the resurrection of those "who sleep in the dust of the earth" and are awakened to everlasting life. The importance here is the expectation being voiced. With the coming of Jesus, God will triumph. In the short time scenario with which Paul is working, everything at the endtimes happens at once. The Lord "will descend from heaven, and the dead in Christ will rise first. Then we who are alive, who are left, will be caught up in the clouds together with them to meet the Lord in the air; and so we will be with the

Lord forever" (1 Thess 4:16-17). (Meeting "in the clouds" recalls Daniel's picture in 7:13.)

No elaborate scheme concerning the endtimes should be made of this, although it assumes an imminent return during the lifetime of Paul and his fellow Christians. More significant is that the victory of God will occur and, to use Daniel's language again: "Many of those who sleep in the dust of the earth shall awake, some to everlasting life" (12:2). The second coming is followed by "eternity," or as Paul puts it, "so we will be with the Lord forever." Being caught up in the air should be taken no more literally than the call of the archangel and the sound of the trumpet. But no more striking imagery can be utilized to describe the indescribable, namely the final victory of God and the people of faith. In the meantime, Paul's words continue to comfort Christians. The emphasis is on God. It is God "through Jesus" whom Paul sees at the endtimes, the God who sent Jesus, and by implication, the God who raises the dead.[1]

"He Appeared . . . Also to Me" (1 Cor 15:5, 8)

So far Paul has made no reference to the resurrection as an historical event. He assumes that Jesus is exalted in heaven and bears witness that Jesus has been revealed in him. Beyond that he does not objectify the resurrection or refer to the empty tomb.

What, then, does Paul say about the resurrection appearances? For the answer to this question, we must turn to 1 Corinthians 15, probably the earliest written references to the resurrection appearances. In this chapter Paul is mainly concerned with belief in the resurrection of the dead. Evidently, questions had been raised in the church about the resurrection of the dead. Paul is obviously at pains to affirm the resurrection of the dead and to say that there is a "spiritual body" because "flesh and blood cannot inherit the kingdom of God"

(15:44, 50). Since it appears that some of the Corinthians were saying, "there is no resurrection of the dead," Paul begins by reminding them that the faith of the first community is based upon the resurrection of Jesus, and therefore "if the dead are not raised, then Christ has not been raised" (v. 16). Paul puts faith in the resurrection of the dead ahead of the resurrection of Jesus.

At the beginning of chapter 15 Paul recites the basic elements of the gospel. He says he has proclaimed to the Corinthians what he also had received: "Christ died for our sins in accordance with the scriptures . . . he was raised on the third day in accordance with the scriptures" (vv. 3-4). Hans Kung in his book *Eternal Life?* says this is "not so much a historical assertion as a theological assertion," and that the selection of the number "three" is symbolic.[2] Whether or not Paul is making a theological assertion remains speculation. He appears to be very straightforward as he gives a list of Christ's appearances to Cephas, the twelve, more than five hundred brothers and sisters, James, all of the apostles, and "last of all . . . also to me" (15:5-9). No doubt, there were those still alive who could "check" his list.

In chapter 15 Paul makes no mention of an empty tomb or of Mary Magdalene and the other women at the tomb. Some scholars suggest that the witness of women in those days was not considered credible, so Paul omitted any mention of Christ's appearances to women. It may simply be that he knew nothing of those appearances.

In his list of appearances Paul uses the Greek word *opthe*, meaning "appeared." It denotes something that happens to someone without their volition. Graham Stanton sees this as referring to more than "subjective conclusions." He believes that a distinction can be drawn between visual appearances and later mystical experiences.[3] In any event, the word suggests that the appearance to Peter and the others, including Paul, was unexpected. Note that Paul gives no description here of an encounter with Jesus, either for himself or the others, just as he gives no description to the Galatians. Undoubtedly the experience was important to Paul, since he bases his authority and apostleship upon it, but he feels no need to give details of his experience. He also claims that his experience is the last of the visual appearances.

In the remainder of chapter 15 Paul's basic affirmation is that God raised Christ (v. 15). With this declaration comes the statement that the exalted Christ reigns: "For he must reign until he has put all his enemies under his feet. The last enemy to be destroyed is death" (vv. 25-26). Paul is making an apocalyptic assumption by affirming the sovereignty of God over all evil, including the final evil—death itself. God's sovereignty reigns. Paul testifies that God raised Jesus; otherwise, as Paul says bluntly, "We are even found to be misrepresenting God, because we testified of God that he raised Christ" (v. 15).

Paul's witness to the exaltation of Jesus is really about the sovereignty of God, which is really the theme of apocalyptic thought. All the great themes of conquering death and of life beyond the grave, hang upon whether or not the first sentence of the Apostles Creed is true: "I believe in God the Father Almighty." The hope for restoration of the people of God and the defeat of God's enemies hinge upon faith in the sovereignty of God.

"Flesh and Blood Cannot Inherit" (1 Cor 15:50)

Although Paul stresses an element of continuity between the buried and raised body of the believer, he does not describe the resurrected body of Jesus or anyone else. He writes only of the physical and spiritual bodies, saying that what is sown is "perishable" and what is raised is "imperishable" (15:42-50).

He sees the exalted Christ as "the first fruits" of "the resurrection of the dead" (vv. 20-21) and as "a life-giving spirit" (v. 45). He promises that "we shall bear the image of the man of heaven" (v. 49), but does not attempt to say what that means.

Finally, he concludes by declaring that "flesh and blood cannot inherit the kingdom of God, nor the perishable inherit the imperishable" (v. 50). Paul flatly refuses to introduce flesh and blood in any description of the resurrected body. He believes that God has raised Jesus as the exalted Christ who will reign until the complete defeat of evil and death. He also believes that Jesus is in heaven interceding for us (Rom 8:34); that is, in the exalted Jesus the imperishable love of God is interceding for us. This love is imperishable because it is not defeated upon any cross. The evil and pain of the world do not have the last word and cannot separate us from the love of God in Christ.

"Therefore" (1 Cor 15:58)

From Paul's witness two things remain to be said, both of which are prefaced by Paul's great "therefore." "Therefore . . . be steadfast" in the faith that God has raised Christ and the decisive battle has been won. The sovereign love of God reigns. Paul waits for the apocalyptic trumpet to sound victory: "We will all be changed, in a moment, in the twinkling of an eye, at the last trumpet. For the trumpet will sound, and the dead will be raised imperishable, and we will be changed" (15:51). Paul does not specify times or indulge in lurid descriptions. He simply affirms that the victory has been won and we wait for the "last trumpet." "We will be changed" suggest hope of eternal life in a dimension beyond human description.

In his second letter to Corinth, Paul expands on the concept of change: "For we know that if the earthly tent we live in is destroyed, we have a building from God, a house not made with hands, eternal in the heavens" (2 Cor 5:1). We will be "away from the body and at home with the Lord" (v. 8). Paul would say that the resurrection of the body does not mean flesh and blood, but he does not deny that the person or the exalted Jesus is lost in some eternal sea. As George Buttrick used to say, "God is not a tinpot God ruling over a graveyard."

This is Paul's witness, both to the resurrection of Jesus and to hope beyond the grave. The hope is that "I" will be "I" and "you" will be "you," but "this mortal body must put on immortality" (1 Cor 15:54). This hope comes from God.

The last "therefore" in Paul's witness concerning the resurrection is the call to faithfulness. "Therefore . . . be steadfast, immovable, always excelling in the work of the Lord, because you know that in the Lord your labor is not in vain" (15:58). This is a call to faithfulness and courage, which is the call of the apocalypticist, as in Daniel and Ezekiel. This call to courage is based on the faith that God has defeated evil. In Christian faith the decisive battle has been fought and won in the death and exaltation of Jesus.

Paul writes of this exaltation in the beautiful "hymn" in Philippians 2. Christ Jesus is seen as having been in the form of God, but emptying himself and taking the form of a slave (2:5-7), becoming obedient to death on the cross. "Therefore God also highly exalted him and gave him the name that is above every name" (v. 9). This hymn may have been written before Paul's ministry began, and if so, it affirms the previous existance of the faith that Jesus was exalted by God.

In writing to the church at Philippi, Paul assumes that Jesus is in heaven (1:21) and feels no need to refer to the resurrection except in terms of the exaltation of Jesus. He expresses a strong desire "to know Christ and the power of his resurrection and the sharing of his sufferings . . . if somehow [he] may attain the resurrection from the dead" (3:10-11). It is Paul's hope that if God has raised Jesus, then he, too, may look forward to that same power. From this hope Paul draws courage, even when he is "utterly, unbearably crushed" and despairs of "life itself" (2 Cor 1:8).

We must assume that Paul's witness to those who formed the community of faith at Philippi was along the same lines we find in his letter to them. If that is so, then his witness concerning the resurrection of Jesus must have been in terms of God exalting Jesus in heaven as an affirmation of the faithful obedience of Jesus in suffering. To the Corinthians he expands this theme and sees Jesus as the exalted and reigning Christ, putting down evil until the victory at the endtimes. In Philippians 2:10 there is more than a hint of this: "At the name of Jesus every knee should bend, in heaven and on earth and under the earth, and every tongue should confess that Jesus Christ is Lord, to the glory of God the Father." This call for confession is immediately followed by a call to faithfulness: "Work out your own salvation with fear and trembling; for it is God at work in you" (vv. 12-13). Near the end of the letter to Philippi, Paul writes that he has learned "the secret of having plenty and of being in need" (4:12). That secret would be in trusting the faithfulness of God, no matter what happens: "I can do all things through him who strengthens me" (4:13). This trust he calls "the peace of God, which surpasses all understanding" (4:7).

Paul's witness to the resurrection carries with it the strong note of apocalyptic courage: "We do not lose heart" (2 Cor 4:16). Great apocalyptic writing was intended for failing hearts. In the face of seemingly overwhelming odds, Daniel declared the victory of God and urged courage upon the dispirited Jews who were still under the heel of tyranny. When the bright vision of Abraham's children was fading in Babylon, Ezekiel promised that God would bring them home. Paul's witness is not concerned with details of the resurrection, the endtimes, or of times and seasons, but with hearing the sound of the trumpet of God's victory.

Although Paul gives no details concerning the resurrection of Jesus, he does not doubt that God has exalted Jesus. He gives no details concerning a resurrection body, either of Jesus or anyone else, yet his faith is firm that life does not end with the grave. He does not elaborate on his own experience. (He was not present at the empty tomb or in the upper room.) He does not find it necessary to dwell on any other issues. Even the Damascus Road experience Luke describes in Acts is remarkably void of details. There is a light and a voice that only Paul hears. "Last of all . . . he appeared also to me" (1 Cor 15:8) The nature of that appearance must remain personal. Details are not necessary. Paul's reticence is important. What details can anyone give who has come to faith in the exalted Christ?

With faith in the exalted Jesus comes faith on a broader scale. What does it really mean to believe that God has raised Jesus? Faith tells us there is certainly life beyond the grave. Details about the end of time and the second coming of Christ are unnecessary. As far as I am concerned, the end of time is when I die. The real question is this: Is there a God who raises the dead? The second coming is secondary. Paul, I believe, would have subscribed to the witness in John's Gospel: "I will come again and will take you to myself" (14:3). Only faith matters. Paul's witness is that at the end of the world the sovereign mercy of God will be there.

Paul does not ask us to believe in the resurrection of Jesus so much as he asks us to believe that nothing can separate us from the love of God (Rom 8:38-39). We have been standing behind or sitting before pulpits for nearly two thousand years wondering if "things present or things to come" can separate us from the love of God. The Jesus to whom Paul witnesses is the Jesus who has shared our sufferings and the one whom God has exalted. This is the essence of apocalyptic faith: when one is upon some cross, one must believe that it will not win. Admittedly, a mere affirmation of this, even if in a loud voice, will not suffice. But personal faith begins here and commits oneself to the God who was in Christ and who has shared our pain. Paul discovered, as we do, that the victory is postponed but not canceled. The sovereign love and mercy of God are beyond this present pain.

Paul and Our Times

As it was in Paul's time, this faith in modern times is cast upon a vast sea of discontent and doubt that evil or personal pain can be overcome. People feel helpless in the face of events.

Guilt abides, but it is no longer understood as rebellion against God. Therefore, grace is neither understood nor appreciated. There is a great void that needs to be filled by faith in an intercession for our weakness. How can the power of apocalyptic faith in the final victory of God be appropriated in a world that sees victory in terms of the power of weapons and material resources? This was Paul's witnessing problem, and it remains today.

This problem remains because faith is thrust almost rudely into a world of continual struggles for power. This battle casts doubt upon all earthly sovereignty and suggests that our weaknesses and transgressions cannot be overcome simply by earthly remedy or even earthly explanation. It calls for other virtues such as patience and endurance. We must understand that we are creatures who must look beyond ourselves for our succor. Paul points to the exalted Christ and the love of God that does not condemn only, but first intercedes for us.

"Who is to condemn? It is Christ Jesus, who died, yes, who was raised, who is at the right hand of God, who indeed intercedes for us" (Rom 8:34). The resurrection-exaltation of Jesus means that something of us intercedes before the throne. It brings its own healing and with that a quality of mercy that bears all things and does not "rejoice in wrongdoing, but rejoices in the truth" (1 Cor 13:6). "For now we see in a mirror, dimly, but then . . ." (v. 12). "But then" is the apocalyptic faith that questions all earthly powers and points to the power of God. "But then" offers something beyond now. So "we do not lose heart."

This trust is what Paul calls "the peace of God, which surpasses all understanding" (Phil 4:7). But it is a peace that is always found in the shadow of a cross, a peace within plenty and want, a peace that speaks to our pain and not our ease. It is also prophetic faith. For if the resurrection is the promise of God's victory, then evil done or complied with is under the judgment of God. "Abounding in the work of the Lord" (1 Cor 15:58 KJV) is not just increasing a pledge to the church. Too many stewardship sermons (including some of my own) have sold this great word too cheaply. Abounding in the work of the Lord is also seeking justice and doing mercy. The peace of God follows faithful obedience.

The resurrection of Jesus also means that we are not called to this rigorous faith alone. The God who raised Jesus is at work in you. Prophetic believing and preaching that call for great efforts toward social justice have as their companion the sovereign God who participates in this kind of work. Facing life's pain is accompanied by the promised companionship of a loving God. Admittedly, all of this is done "with fear and trembling" (Phil 2:12-13).

Apocalyptic faith listens for "the archangel's call and the sound of God's trumpet" (1 Thess 4:16). Great apocalyptic writing, such as Daniel or Ezekiel or Paul, was directed to failing hearts. In the face of seemingly overwhelming odds Daniel declared the victory of God and urged courage upon the dispirited Jews who were under the heel of tyranny. When the bright vision of Abraham's children was fading in Babylon, Ezekiel promised that God would bring them home. In the first century (and now) there were those who believed they had been raised from the stones (Matt 3:9) as Abraham's children. When they found their hearts failing, Paul assured them: "If we have been united with him in a death like his, we will certainly be united with him in a resurrection like his" (Rom 6:5).

Notes

[1]In regard to this matter of the endtimes, what are we really saying? For some, the endtime is seen in decidedly realistic and literal terms of a kingdom of God on earth, to which is attached the idea of a "millennium" gathered from Revelation 20. Jesus spoke of an endtime, but was careful not to speak in terms of times and seasons or even in any literal millennium. He was an apocalypticist in that he saw God triumphing in the end. There is no doubt that the Gospel writers and early Christians believed in the final triumph, although they finally came to the conclusion that it might not happen in their lifetime. They did, however, embrace belief in the triumph of God

over evil. That triumph might occur within time or beyond time. For example, John, in the book of Revelation, looked for the final defeat of Rome.

[2]In regard to the resurrection of Jesus as an "historical event," the reader should note Hans Kung's *Eternal Life?* (Garden City NY: Doubleday & Co., 1984) ch. 5, and the section on "the earliest Easter testimony." Kung draws a distinction between the resurrection as an "historical event" and a "real event." He does not see the resurrection as "an event in space and time," but as a "real event" for those who commit themselves to it "in reasonable trust" (or faith?). The apostle Paul referred to the resurrection of Jesus as a "real event." Drawing the distinction between "historical" and "real" relieves one from the necessity of proving a historical event. But Paul's list of those to whom Jesus "appeared" would seem to be both "historical" and "real." The nature of those appearances is the problem, especially in reading the Gospels. On the whole topic of appearances, see J. D. G. Dunn, *Jesus and the Spirit* (Philadelphia: Westminster, 1975) ch. 5.

[3]The problem of understanding and translating *opthe* is not simple. The *Oxford Greek Dictionary*, for example, sees the word as referring to metaphorical or mental sight, in the sense of "discern" or "perceive," as in Sophocles' *Electra*, line 945. In John 16:16, "You will see me," the question may be raised as to whether this is sensual or mental perception. Is this encounter with Jesus taking place in faith under the power of the Holy Spirit? Graham Stanton's comments quoted in this chapter are worthy of note in this connection. In regard to the general question of the resurrection, two recent books should be noted: Stanton, *Gospel Truth? New Light on Jesus and the Gospels* (London: HarperCollins, 1995), and Stephen Barton and Graham Stanton, ed. *Resurrection* (London: SPCK, 1994).

CHAPTER 3

THE GREAT SURPRISE IN MARK

Of the four Gospels, Mark places us closest to the witness of the early communities of faith and to the earliest written tradition concerning the scene at the empty tomb.[1] Evidently, from the beginning he knows—and we must assume believes—the story of the empty tomb. Tradition has it that his Gospel represents the witness of the apostle Peter. The actual author of the Gospel is unknown, but it is believed he wrote from Rome, sometime shortly before or after the fall of Jerusalem in 70 CE.

"I Know Who You Are" (1:24)

Mark begins his story with Jesus as an adult power figure. He is announced as the Son of God. John the Baptizer comes on the scene immediately to point to Jesus as the Messiah. Next we are taken to the baptism and hear the voice from heaven: "You are my Son, the Beloved" (1:11). The temptation follows, but without details. Jesus' triumph over Satan is assumed and underscored by the presence of angels ministering to him (1:13). Mark continues to show Jesus being recognized as a power figure even by unclean spirits and demons: "I know who you are, the Holy One of God" (1:24). Jesus shows his power by casting out the unclean spirit. His authority is recognized with amazement.

Mark then recites numerous healings and exorcisms. The healing of the paralytic brings forth the question, "Who can forgive sins but God alone?" (2:12) Jesus' authority over the Hebrew Sabbath is affirmed (2:27). The demoniac is healed, and Jairus' daughter is raised. An unknown woman touches his garment and is healed. His authority is given to the twelve, and they are sent out to preach that the kingdom-rule of God is at hand. By that authority they cast out demons and heal the sick.

This Gospel account comes from disciples who clearly do not understand Jesus' mission. At one point his mother and brothers appear to bring him home, suggesting that he is mad (3:31). The stilling of the storm (4:35-41) results in the question from the disciples: "Who then is this?" Something has happened to this community that will later project a powerful witness and will find its way into the final pages of Mark's Gospel. His sayings and deeds are now remembered and understood in that light.

"When He Comes in the Glory" (8:29–9:1)

Mark's story is projected to the end and beyond. Peter declares that Jesus is the Messiah. The disciples hear the teaching concerning the necessity of the suffering of the Messiah, but they do not understand. Jesus makes his call for disciplined faithfulness with words about self-denial and taking up a cross. "Those who are ashamed of me and of my words in this adulterous and sinful generation, of them the Son of Man will also be ashamed when he comes in the glory of his Father with the holy angels" (8:38). Here apocalyptic imagery denotes the final triumph and judgment of God. Scholars continue to differ over whether or not he saw himself as that Son of man. Scholars debate the claim that Jesus was a full-blown apocalypticist, but it is clear his message was basically apocalyptic. As Bart D. Ehrman observes, "It is probably safe to say that all of

[Jesus'] followers had accepted Jesus' basic apocalyptic message while he was still alive."[2]

By the time of Mark and his readers, the end had not yet come. The author of this Gospel knew that and so did his readers. But then Jesus says: "Truly, I tell you, there are some standing here who will not taste death until they see that the kingdom of God has come with power" (9:1). According to Mark and the other Gospel writers, the disciples affirmed Jesus as the Christ, but had no real understanding of the suffering Christ or of the victory God would have through him. Prior to the empty tomb, they are reported as having received this kind of instruction, but only afterward are shown to believe and understand. They had seen the kingdom of God come with power in Jesus' death and exaltation. They had also seen it in the subsequent power of their witness.

"From the Four Winds" (13:27)

There was a kingdom that did not come—the restored kingdom of Israel. When Jesus enters Jerusalem, the crowds cry out: "Hosanna! Blessed is the one who comes in the name of the Lord! Blessed is the kingdom of our ancestor David! Hosanna in the highest heaven!" (11:9-10) The cry was voicing the expectation that one of David's line would again sit on the throne and restore the kingdom to Israel. But that kingdom did not come when Jesus entered Jerusalem or afterward. Mark says nothing more about a kingdom restored to Israel. Instead, he gives us the little apocalypse in chapter 13. It is a mixture of two times: (1) the destruction of Jerusalem, and (2) a time that is beyond time, when the angels will gather the "elect from the four winds, from the ends of the earth to the ends of heaven" (13:27).

The scene is outside the Temple. Jesus points to that great structure and says the time will come when there will not be left one stone upon another. He foresees the eventual destruction of Jerusalem and the Temple by the Romans, which happened in 70 CE. All signs were pointing toward the time when Rome's patience would end with these troublesome Jews. As Jesus warns of the coming destruction, he warns against thinking that the end will also come. (Interestingly, the restoration of a Jewish kingdom is omitted in this discourse.) The disciples are not to be led astray by false messiahs. Neither are they to be alarmed by "wars and rumors of wars," which is the stuff of history, as are earthquakes and famines. Disciples must expect to be persecuted for their faithfulness, but they are to remain steady in the face of it. Jesus counsels that they are to flee for their lives when the destruction is near. (Tradition has it that the Christians in Jerusalem took this advice as the Roman armies approached, shortly before 70 CE.) Still they are not to be led astray by false messiahs, and assume the end is near.[3]

Then the tone and direction change. Jesus begins to speak of something happening "after that suffering" (13:24). The language becomes decidedly apocalyptic: "The sun will be darkened, and the moon will not give its light, and the stars will be falling from heaven, and the powers in the heaven will be shaken" (13:24-26). Such language and imagery are not to be taken literally. Rather, it should be read as pointing toward the final victory and judgment of God: "And then they will see 'the Son of man coming in clouds' with great power and glory. Then he will send out the angels, and gather his elect from the four winds, from the ends of the earth to the ends of heaven" (13:26-27). This apocalyptic imagery is reminiscent of the picture in Daniel 7:13, a situation beyond the constraints of time. Even if it does not happen in their time, the disciples are called to live in faith and expectation.[4] that wrong may seem forever on the throne, and truth forever on the scaffold, as James Russell Lowell put it in his poem "The Present Crisis":

> Yet that scaffold sways the future,
> And behind the dim unknown
> Standeth God within the shadows,
> Keeping watch above his own.[5]

Up to chapter 12, Jesus is presented as the power figure. Nothing seems too great for him. In chapter 13, however, it seems that history and time have slipped beyond Jesus. He stands seemingly helpless before the coming forces that will destroy Jerusalem and the Temple. He speaks of wars and rumors of wars, nations rising against nation, earthquakes and famines, as though these things will not only happen, but that they will happen and God will not move. In short, he assumes the continuing power of evil to inflict pain upon the earth. His only counsel is to stand faithful and not be led astray by false messiahs. Then he moves rapidly toward the "end," the coming of the Son of man "with great glory and power" and the promise of victory at the end. His counsel is, "Beware, keep alert; for you do not know when the time will come" (13:33). We cannot speculate about whether or not Jesus expected this to happen in his lifetime.

"The Son of Man Goes" (14:21)

The apocalyptic call to faith is now carried forward to the night when he was betrayed. We are shown a scene of sorrow: "For the Son of man goes as it is written of him" (14:21).[6] He is no longer a power figure. He speaks of betrayal. In Gethsemane he admits that his soul is "deeply grieved, even to death" (14:34). His prayer is for the cup to pass. Then there is the final word of resignation: "The Son of man is betrayed into the hands of sinners" (14:41). According to Mark, the powerful Danielic figure of the Son of man is reduced to betrayal "into the hands of sinners," and there are no angels to blow God's trumpets of victory. All the apocalyptic imagery of victory is stripped away. We are left with the seeming victory of evil. Disciples vanish.

One figure remains. Although his power and authority seem to have vanished, Mark sketches a majesty about him, while he stands before his judges. The majesty is silent, except for one moment. The high priest asks the question: "Are you the Messiah, the Son of the Blessed One?" (14:61) Whatever motive the high priest may have had, this is the pivotal question. Again, scholars differ as to whether or not these words have been put in the mouth of Jesus. Nevertheless, the answer needs to be given: "I am; and 'you will see the Son of man seated at the right hand of the Power, and 'coming with the clouds of heaven' " (14:62). If there is a moment when faith in God's power must be affirmed, this is the moment. The answer that Mark says Jesus gave is an affirmation of that power. Is God still on the throne or not? At this moment in time, when the good stands before destruction, is the throne empty? Is there no sovereignty greater than this moment of darkness? At this moment a statement must be made. Attention must be paid.

If God does not have the final victory, the evil that makes crosses has won. The call to faithfulness becomes hollow. That moment of darkness and defeat is just that, and no more. Did Jesus choose this moment to declare himself? Did he choose this moment to declare the final victory of God?

"A Young Man, Dressed in a White Robe" (16:5)

The Gospels tell us that what was found at the tomb is not what was anticipated. The tomb is unexpectedly empty. As Mary Magdalene, Mary the mother of James, and Salome (16:1) approach the tomb, their conversation anticipates the problem of the stone. "When they looked up, they saw that the stone . . . had been rolled back. . . . they saw a young man, dressed in a white robe, sitting on the right side; and they were alarmed" (16:4-5). The young man in white announces: "He has been raised; he is not here" (16:6). Who is this young man in white? In Matthew his place will be taken by an angel, in Luke there are "two men in dazzling clothes" (24:4), and in John there appear "two angels in white" (20:12). In each Gospel they announce: "He is risen." The tomb stands empty. Did disciples steal the body and place it elsewhere?

There was a tradition circulating in the first century that this was the case, but this explanation will not stand in the light of their subsequent actions. The tomb stands empty. Enter Mark's "young man dressed in a white robe" and his counterparts in the other Gospels. By placing them at the empty tomb, what is being said by the Gospel writers? In apocalyptic language and imagery, angels are messengers of God announcing God's purpose or something God has done or will do. In the Gospels they arrive to explain the empty tomb. So then, is Mark's "young man dressed in a white robe" a muted apocalyptic messenger? His Gentile readers would hardly understand apocalyptic angels. In any event, the first witnesses stand in surprise. The surprise is that God has done something totally unexpected and that act of God changes everything.

The Gospel closest to the early community gives no appearances, only a suggestion of Jesus going before them into Galilee (16:7). Mark chooses to close with the surprise of the empty tomb and the announcement of the "young man dressed in a white robe": "He has been raised; he is not here" (16:6). With restrained simplicity, Mark places the surprise of the empty tomb over against the cross and the apparent triumph of evil. After the stories of the power figure comes the cross. After the assertions of his authority, he is condemned by Roman authority. Now against this Mark sets the empty tomb, as though this is enough. There are no appearances of Jesus and no scenes in the upper room. Angels or men in white who appear in the other Gospels are not here.

The Gospel closest to the early community ends with the first witnesses of the empty tomb leaving in astonishment and fear. The surprise of the empty tomb will become the faith that God has exalted Jesus. It is this faith that will give credence to the gospel story of Jesus, and power to the gospel witness. Now the story is read as written in the light of the empty tomb. The unclean spirits were right! Jesus is the Son of man who has authority on earth to forgive sins. The Sabbath is made for humankind. The true kindred of Jesus are faithful disciples.

The greatest is one who serves. The kingdom-rule of God has come in him with power and will finally be triumphant.

How long did it take for the first communities to arrive at the Easter faith? Perhaps the answer is simple: They accepted Jesus' apocalyptic view of the triumph of God, and they believed that God had not abandoned Jesus, and that Jesus and what he was had not been allowed to fall to the ground. Was it, as Käsemann suggests, by "the experience of the Spirit after Easter"?[7] He is the Son of man who is now exalted and will be exalted at the end. He is the Messiah who suffers, but the suffering itself is exalted and transformed.

Here we must pause and look at where we are. Mark is thought to be the first Gospel written. Behind Mark there is nothing but an oral tradition of some forty years. Of course, in Acts, Luke gives us a small window into the first community, but this is even farther away from that time, in the latter part of the first century. When Mark reports the resurrection, he is writing out of whatever oral tradition came to him. As far as we know, the apostles have faded from the scene. Concerning the resurrection of Jesus, Mark is restrained, an empty tomb and "a young man dressed in a white robe" announcing that he is risen. But according to Mark, that was enough to underpin all he had written before and to affirm the authority of the gospel. From what witness, then, was he writing? As we try to press back to those of the first community, the witness Mark hears is the witness to an empty tomb. The "young man dressed in a white robe" suggests an apocalyptic witness to the triumph of God. Mark leaves it at that and asks us to read his Gospel in that light.

Resurrection Faith-Language

Witness to the cosmic faith in the resurrection requires the strongest kind of language and imagery. Apocalyptic language and imagery are the strongest kind of faith-language that can be used. Mark uses it, although with restraint. There is the little apocalypse in chapter 13, the apocalyptic answer given to the high priest, and the "young man dressed in a white robe" making his announcement before an empty tomb. So again we must ask: What kind of oral witness is Mark drawing upon that requires him to use this language, particularly at a time in the first century when Christians were not always comfortable with apocalypticism, and they expected an immediate end? The conclusion must be that he is drawing upon an apocalyptic faith witness.

It is believed that Mark's Gospel may have been written from Rome and addressed to Christians under persecution there. The story he tells requires a faith-response in the face of a hostile world. What kind of faith-response? Let us imagine a witness without Bibles or churches by a believer who had never seen the empty tomb or been in the upper room. To begin, there would be the faith-witness that God had raised Jesus. Who is Jesus? The witness would answer with stories and words the Gospel writers record. But was not this good man killed? Yes, but not defeated. God has exalted him. Do you mean that it is possible to believe in God and to believe that God can be trusted, that evil does not have the last word? Yes. And not only that, but also the forgiveness of sins is possible. Out of the sufferings and death of Jesus we have found the love of God, and the exaltation of Jesus promises victory over evil at the end. What must I do in the meantime? We are called, replies the witness, to a lifestyle of faithfulness. The witness might use words such as the following:

> We boast in our sufferings. (Rom 5:3)
>
> Believe on the Lord Jesus, and you will be saved. (Acts 16:31)
>
> Be steadfast, unmovable . . . because you know that in the Lord your labor is not in vain. (1 Cor 15:58)
>
> For I am convinced that neither death, nor life, . . . nor anything else in all creation, will be able to separate us from the love of God in Christ Jesus our Lord. (Rom 8:38-39)

What other kind of response did Mark expect from his Gospel with its great surprise of the empty tomb?

Resurrection faith-language, especially apocalyptic language, is the language of victory. For example, telling us to "rejoice" in our sufferings tells us nothing, unless we are told where the "joy" is found. The beginning of resurrection faith-language (and the "joy") is in the faith that God may be trusted to the end of my world or this planet, and that there is no evil greater than God, not even the cross of Jesus. This is the heart of apocalyptic faith *and* the heart of resurrection faith. This faith cannot be defined or its power measured until it meets the pain and doubt, and shapes that pain and doubt into something else. It cannot be defined or measured until it is allowed to meet the challenge of evil and face down evil's assertion of victory. It cannot be measured or defined until it reaches into the heart with the promise of the forgiveness and love of God. Mark's young man in white challenges us with that resurrection faith when he announces to all who approach the unexpected empty tomb: "He has been raised."

The challenge cannot be softened. Mark ends his Gospel with the empty tomb and the announcement. He challenges the faith of his readers. They are called to faithfulness, even when God's victory seems extremely remote and when there is no assurance that God is within the shadows, keeping watch above his own. Recall that incomparable scene with Jesus before the high priest. One joins this scene and stands between despair and hope. Mark brings us into that scene as neither a moment of triumph nor a moment of defeat. This is where Peter stood when his faith buckled and he denied Jesus. Is there a sovereignty of love, mercy, and justice that is greater than this? Or must this scene be played out again and again, where evil's flag is highest and there is no visible redemption coming on clouds of heaven? Mark leaves his readers standing between defeat and victory, between despair and hope. So the final scene in Mark's Gospel is the picture of women fleeing in fear before the great surprise of the empty tomb.

What is this hard word of apocalyptic faith? If Mark wrote his Gospel for the Christians at Rome who were facing persecution, how would they read this? The Son of man does not appear above Rome with power and great glory. The Son of man does not appear anywhere that any of us can see. It is a hard word. There is no softening of it, except by those who wish to present faith as something that can wear soft clothing and live in king's houses (Matt 11:8).

Notes

[1]I am assuming Mark's date to be either just before or just after the fall of Jerusalem in 70 CE. If there is an earlier written tradition, it has not come to light, the assertion that Q is the earliest Gospel notwithstanding. If there is a "proto-Mark," we must assume it would look something like the Gospel we have at present.

[2]See Bart D. Ehrman *The New Testament: A Historical Perspective* (Oxford: Oxford University Press) 234. See also Ernst Käsemann, *New Testament Questions of Today* (London: SCM Press Ltd, 1969) 61, who concludes that the early community was "an orthodox community with a highly strung apocalyptic and messianic hope" (17). Käsemann also writes of "apocalyptic themes forming the real beginning of primitive Christian theology" (102). According to Pheme Perkins, in *Resurrection, New Testament Witness, and Contemporary Reflection* (Garden City NY: Doubleday and Co., 1984) 23, "One finds Christians combining the apocalyptic code of divine victory at the parousia with the belief that the victory over death has been accomplished."

[3]See Perkins.

[4]The "end" is never clearly defined in the New Testament nor in the teachings of Jesus recorded there. It may refer to the "end of time" or to the defeat of some present evil. We cannot use the term in any definitive way, for we are trying to speak of something that may be beyond time, for which there are no descriptive words. The reticence of Jesus here should be emulated.

[5]From *Essays, Poems, and Letters* (Boston: Houghton Mifflin and Co., 1984) 292.

[6]"As it is written of him" may be Mark's commentary. Where he finds it "written" of the Son of Man is not clear. It was much later that the church began to read Isaiah 53 as referring to Jesus as the Suffering Servant. But the servant poems in Isaiah make no reference to the Son of Man. Certainly, the early church came to believe in the necessity of the sufferings of Jesus. Paul, of course, carried this theme to its ultimate.

[6]See Käsemann.

CHAPTER 4

THE REVELATORY MOMENT IN MATTHEW

The language and imagery in the last two chapters of Matthew's Gospel have to be read with some wonderment. Following the death of Jesus, the curtain of the Temple is torn from top to bottom by an invisible hand. There is an earthquake, and rocks are split. Then Matthew says, "The tombs also were opened, and many bodies of the saints who had fallen asleep were raised. After his resurrection they came out of the tombs and entered the holy city and appeared to many" (27:52-53). An angel descends from heaven and rolls back the stone from the tomb and sits on it. Mary Magdalene and the other Mary come upon this scene in fear. The guards are so fearful, they shake and become "like dead men." The angel is "like lightning, and his clothing white as snow."

This is quite an enhancement from the scene Mark presents. The "young man dressed in a white robe" has been transformed into an angel whose "clothing is white as snow." Mark does not mention earthquakes or saints rising from their graves. What can this imagery mean, particularly to modern-day readers and hearers? How can this imagery be presented without straining the credulity of the hearers? Perhaps Matthew may have been pressing the language and imagery to stress the resurrection of Jesus. I suggest he is using apocalyptic imagery to convey what faith sees as an event of great power, an event that has momentous and even cosmic consequences.

"Truly This Man Was God's Son" (27:54)

The language and imagery used in these scenes—earthquakes, an angel making an announcement, tombs being opened—is to be read as apocalyptic language and not taken literally. First-century readers may have been familiar with such language and what it was intended to convey, but twentieth-century readers and hearers are not, although we can understand the message or truth behind the language.

What, then, is the truth behind this language? An unlikely person makes the announcement of the truth of this event. Following the tearing of the curtain of the Temple, the earthquake, and saints coming out of their tombs, a Roman centurion makes an announcement: "Truly this man was God's son" (27:54). That is, the one who has just died is declared the son of God. He is not seen hanging in defeat. The apocalyptic language and imagery point to the magnitude of what is happening. Instead of being taken literally, the language is intended to convey a greater truth concerning what is happening. That truth is declared by the Roman centurion.

The profound truth expressed in the Gospels is that God has raised Jesus, the son of God, and not a hanged criminal. The work of the angel in rolling back the stone indicates the work of God. God is faithful; Jesus has not been abandoned. The announcement of the centurion, accompanied by an earthquake, should be taken together with the announcement of the angel before the tomb: "He is not here; for he has been raised" (28:6).

The women leave the empty tomb "with fear and great joy" (28:8). Joy has been added to Mark's "terror and amazement." They experience the risen Jesus, but we are not given any details, except that "Jesus met them" (28:9). The appearance of Jesus is not described. We are looking at a brief tableau frozen in time, a picture of an experience beyond description. We can say that for the women, it is a revelatory moment. For the remainder of the community, the moments are yet to come.[1]

According to Matthew, that moment comes in Galilee, on "the mountain to which Jesus had directed them" (28:16). This final scene is also an abbreviated scene with Jesus and the Eleven. "When they saw him, they worshiped him; but some doubted" (28:17). Who were the doubters? Were they disciples outside the Eleven? This admission that some doubted, together with "doubting Thomas," is intriguing. What does it suggest? What did the doubters doubt? Was it what they were seeing or experiencing?

There is no way to know, but it does suggest that the earliest experience of some in the first community was mixed, in that there was not immediate and unanimous agreement concerning the resurrection of Jesus. One thing is clear from Matthew's account: The one whom the women and the disciples experience is the same Jesus whom they had known in life. This is the heart of the revelatory moment: The Jesus of "the story," the man of earth, risen and exalted, is the same Jesus.

Matthew gives much importance to what we know as the Great Commission (28:18-20). Disciples are to go and make disciples of all nations, baptizing and teaching in the name of the Father, Son, and Holy Spirit. The later church of Matthew's time (perhaps 80–90 CE) needed to hear this enlarged commission, since the return of Jesus seemed indefinitely delayed. This commission is now strengthened as being given in the name of the Trinity.[2] The church is to witness to the exalted man of earth, the son of God. Their faith-experience, following the empty tomb, was that God had not abandoned Jesus, but that Jesus had been exalted by God. Neither Matthew nor Mark indicate an ascension. Both suggest an experience that began with the women and then included the inner circle of the Eleven. According to Matthew, that experience is coupled with the great commission. No "forty days" follows, as in Acts.

Easter without the great commission leaves the hearers with nothing more to do than to wait for immortality and to stand gazing up into heaven. If God has not abandoned Jesus, then there is a message to be proclaimed and work to be done. If all authority has been given to the exalted Christ by God, that great moment must be proclaimed with earthquakes, an angel sitting upon the stone, together with a Roman centurion declaring him to be the son of God. Matthew would proclaim that in nothing less than apocalyptic language. What a cast—an angel sitting on a stone, a Roman centurion, Mary Magdalene (of once doubtful reputation?), some doubting disciples, accompanied by earthquakes and the rocks of the earth being split! And with all that a monumental work to be done, giving enough meaning to life for a hundred lifetimes.

"God Is with Us" (1:23)

Matthew opens and closes his Gospel with the promise of Emmanuel. In the opening of the Gospel, "an angel of the Lord appeared to [Joseph] in a dream" (1:20), announcing God's intentions and instructing Joseph to "take Mary as your wife, for the child conceived in her is from the Holy Spirit. She will bear a son, and you are to name him Jesus, for he will save his people from their sins" (1:20-21). Matthew then adds: "All this took place to fulfill what had been spoken by the Lord through the prophet: 'Look, a virgin shall conceive and bear a son, and they shall name him Emmanuel" (1:22-23). Then Matthew thinks it important that we understand the meaning of the name, for he adds: "which means, 'God is with us' " (1:23). The name is most important, for it carries with it the promise of the saving presence of God. Matthew then closes his Gospel with the same promise of the saving presence of God in Jesus: "And remember, I am with you always, to the end of the age" (28:20).

Matthew, quoting from Isaiah 7:14, takes us back to that time when Isaiah was trying to persuade Ahaz, king of Judah, to trust the Lord when danger threatened. In the original context of events, Isaiah was saying that God is with them (Emmanuel) in saving power, if they will turn and trust. Matthew brings that ancient assurance forward and places it over the birth of Jesus and again following the death of Jesus. For him, Jesus is Emmanuel, God with us in saving power. Later, John in his Gospel gives his own birth story in terms of the Word becoming flesh and dwelling among us, giving power to become children of God (John 1:12). Both evangelists convey the same faith. In Jesus, God is with us in saving power. In Matthew, it is the apocalyptic angel who makes this announcement and who appears again to declare the exaltation of Jesus and the faithfulness of God (28:2). There is another promise of the presence in Matthew 18:20: "For where two or three are gathered in my name, I am there among them."

"If You Are the Son of God" (4:3)

Apocalyptic imagery is always a call to faith. From the beginning to the end of Jesus' earthly ministry, the issue is faith. At his baptism a "voice from heaven" announces, "This is my Son, the Beloved" (3:17), and in his last days the Roman centurion declares Jesus to be "God's Son." Likewise, the temptation follows this identification. The Son faces one supreme temptation—to press God's faithfulness to the extreme. The devil tests Jesus by saying, "If you are the Son of God, . . . command these stones to become loaves of bread. . . . throw yourself down [from the pinnacle of the Temple]. . . . accept evil in order to gain the kingdoms of the world" (paraphrased). Jesus resists by affirming the sovereignty of God and refusing to press that sovereignty to the extreme: "Do not put the Lord your God to the test" (4:7). What is the ultimate temptation Jesus refuses?

The answer is in the remainder of Matthew and also in the other Gospels. Jesus' faith-obedience carries him to the cross, where that faith-obedience is tested to the extreme. The real temptation is to avoid the cross, to avoid suffering and death, to avoid placing everything on the line in faith-obedience. At the end it would appear that evil has won, but not so. An angel comes and sits upon a stone in front of an empty tomb.

"Until the Harvest" (13:30)

This faith-obedience is to endure to the end. According to Matthew (and also Mark 1:15), Jesus comes preaching, "Repent, for the kingdom of heaven has come near" (4:17). That is, God's kingdom or rule is at hand. We are called to respond to the sovereign rule of God and to repent. The word "repent" needs to be preached and understood as turning and responding to God's rule. Jesus comes preaching the ancient message of the prophets before him. God is ruling. Turn and respond to that rule. And that response in faith-obedience is to be to the end—whenever that will be.

But unless God is both sovereign and faithful, of what use is faith or joining the battle against evil? Maybe it is better to accept evil and gain all the kingdoms of the world; to practice reckless faith by demanding more of that faithful sovereignty than may be granted; to require that God turn stones into bread before you will believe. If not that, then what is left. Turn and respond to God's faithful rule, even if it means a cross; even if the stones do not turn to bread. That, I suggest, is repentance.

Certainly this kind of trust is painful. Not only are we not promised immunity from pain, but we also may have to watch the evil continue along with the good. Jesus explained it this way: "Not one [sparrow] will fall to the ground apart from your Father" (10:29). Daniel and Ezekiel would respond likewise. The fight is long; the pain continues; the sparrow falls. But God promises to "bring you back . . . from your graves" (Ezek 37:12-13).

The other word from Jesus is equally painful, perhaps more so: "Let both of them grow together until the harvest" (13:30).

The weeds must grow along with the good grain. The enemy keeps coming and sowing weeds. Why? And why do the weeds grow and choke out the good? The weeds do grow, even in my own heart. "Let both of them grow together." This is a painful word—painful to hear, painful to endure, and certainly painful to preach. "Let both of them grow together until the harvest," even when there is really no good answer as to why—or when.

Here we are fully into the apocalyptic theme of faithfulness in the face of evil. Believing and preaching this word of Jesus is a call to faith and patience, and it is one with Ezekiel and Daniel: "Let them both grow together until the harvest; and at harvest time I will tell the reapers, 'Collect the weeds first and bind them in bundles to be burned, but gather the wheat into my barn' "(13:30). The apocalyptic faith is that there will be a harvest. The evil will be destroyed completely. The wheat will remain, even as John in Revelation sees the souls of the martyrs safe "under the altar" of God (Rev 6:9); or as Daniel sees the resurrection of the just (12:2), and John in his Gospel sees the light not overcome by the darkness (1:5).

"When the Son of Man Comes in His Glory" (25:31)

The harvest, the light not being overcome by the darkness, the triumph of God—all these expressions come to focus in the fullest apocalyptic passage in Matthew 25:31-46: "When the Son of man comes in his glory, and all the angels with him, then he will sit on the throne of his glory" (25:31). After the parable of the weeds growing until the harvest, Jesus calls for the denial of self and taking up a cross: "For the Son of Man is to come with his angels in the glory of his Father, and then he will repay everyone for what has been done" (16:27).

The reference to the Son of man coming in glory reflects Daniel 7:9-14. Before the great throne of the Ancient One, "one like a human being" is presented, and "to him was given dominion and glory and kingship" (v. 14). Is this a person, or is it a figure representative of the triumph of God's people? I suggest it is both. Jesus uses it in the context of future triumph, as in the harvest scene in the parable. It is part of the apocalyptic assurance we have already seen in the Hebrew Scriptures.[3]

The picture of the great judgment scene in Matthew 25 should be read in this light. The Son of man comes in his glory. The sheep and goats are separated, as are the wheat and tares. Commendation is given to those who minister to "the least of these who are members of my family," and judgment is pronounced on those who do not. But who are these? And who are "all the nations" gathered before the king? There are two views.

"All the nations" may be a universal reference, including those who fail to minister to the needy, hungry, and imprisoned. Those who take this view see here the great emphasis on social justice joined to the apocalyptic faith that good will triumph. The faithful may refer to those who minister to the sick and imprisoned and let both wheat and tares grow until the harvest comes—in faith that there will be a harvest. They have joined the battle, believing that God is faithful and their struggle is not in vain. This view strongly suggests that the faithful are not simply called to wait for God to do something, but they have a part in the battle whose outcome they believe is assured. A Christian hymn by William Walsham How catches this faith:

> And when the strife is fierce, the warfare long,
> Steals on the ear the distant triumph song,
> And hearts are brave again, and arms are strong.

This is all well and good, and I personally like this view very much, but there is another view. "The least of these who are members of my family" may refer to the disciples of Jesus who suffer because of their faith. This is assurance that their persecutors ("all the nations") will one day face the Son of man in his glory and triumph. In the meantime, disciples are encouraged to hold on to their faith and to remain faithful in the face of whatever comes to them.

I prefer to consolidate these views because I do not want to lose the strong call for universal human compassion and love to the needy, sick, hungry, and imprisoned of the earth. If the Christians of Matthew's time heard this as the assurance that their sufferings would one day be judged by the triumphant Son of man, why not? If, on the other hand, this call for compassion and love extends to suffering Christians, why would Christians not be called upon to extend that compassion to one another and to everyone? If Christ as the Son of man is seen identifying himself with his suffering followers, why not with everyone? The one constant here is the triumph of the Son of man and the continuing apocalyptic promise of the victory of God.

One more word about this scene: It is both "then" and "now." It is "then" in that we hear it as something for the end. It is also "now." An angel sits upon a stone before an empty tomb *now*. Christ is risen *now*. The exalted Christ reigns *now*. God is faithful *now*. Sheep and goats make their fateful decision before the imprisoned, hungry, and naked of the world *now*. The Son of man sits upon the throne of his glory *now*. "We are God's children *now*; what we will be has not yet been revealed" (1 John 3:2). The concepts of "now" and "then" are also heard at the empty tomb, where we are beyond space and time, and angels roll away stones.[4]

"When I Drink It New with You" (26:29)

Finally, we move with Matthew to the last night and the last supper. There is the promise: "I will never again drink of this fruit of the vine until that day when I drink it new with you in my Father's kingdom" (26:29). This is both now and then, end and beginning, denouement and anticipation. "I will never again drink of this fruit of the vine"—this is the end of the story of the man of earth. "Until that day when I drink it new with you in my Father's kingdom"—this is anticipation, beyond time and space, a reaching forward beyond the immediate darkness. It is also the essence of apocalyptic faith. When we celebrate the sacrament of the Lord's Supper, we are present on the night when he was betrayed. Yet we do not take the cup believing the enemy has won. We hear only the words "until that day when I drink it new with you." Now we hear in the anticipation of victory. We drink in faith that the tomb is empty and God is faithful. There is one of our flesh before the throne who was called Emmanuel, God with us to the close of the age.

Believing in the apocalyptic resurrection of Jesus is inextricably coupled with the Great Commission. Since Matthew's time the church has waited and realized that the end has not come. Millennia have come and gone. Another millennium is upon us. The end is not yet. But there remains this command: "Go . . . make disciples of all nations." This is what Christians heard at the end of the first millennium. This is an evangelistic call; there are disciples to be made. But there is also justice waiting to be done, the hungry to be fed, and the naked clothed. But by what authority? That mission is prefaced by "all authority in heaven and on earth has been given to me." Recall Paul's words "he must reign until . . ." (1 Cor 15:25). Churches are great about drawing up mission statements, but upon what authority do they base them? Everything the church does must be centered around the authority of the reigning Christ and the promise of Emmanuel.

Communion needs to be set in this cosmic apocalyptic faith. When the cup is taken, even at the darkest of times in the soul or in the world, there is the promise that it will yet be taken new in the Father's kingdom. Whatever we bring to the Table, it cannot separate us from the love of God, and it is not greater than the saving power of Emmanuel.

The Requirement of Apocalyptic Faith

Apocalyptic faith requires that we believe and live both in time and beyond time.[5] The preacher stands in time in the pulpit and has a precious few minutes to proclaim something that is beyond space and time, but also that can touch every soul within the sound of the preacher's voice. What a marvelous place to stand! Where angels roll away stones and announce God's faithfulness and victory to every person who is fighting a battle.

Of course, believing that God is with us is a comforting theme, especially at Advent and Christmas. It takes on greater power when it is proclaimed and believed in the light of the faithfulness of God in raising Jesus. Indeed, it is in the light of that exaltation that Matthew wrote his Gospel. The promise of the saving presence is undergirded by the faith that God can be trusted. The birth of Jesus has meaning because the death of Jesus was not the end. Otherwise, Christmas becomes a sentiment that passes when the last candle and the lights are removed from the tree. Somewhere in our celebration there ought to be a place for earthquakes, rocks being split, and apocalyptic angels.

I began with Matthew's Gospel by asking how we can believe his apocalyptic imagery. I end by suggesting that we should celebrate that imagery, which is what Matthew is asking us to do. That imagery in the hands of the preacher can make the sermon of great event and power. And for those of us who read this Gospel seeking to strengthen our faith, Matthew does not ask us to strain our credulity. He is reminding us that the magnitude of the resurrection calls for nothing short of angels sitting on a stone before an empty tomb.

Notes

[1]I am indebted to a colleague at Queens College for suggesting the phrase "apocalyptic moments." Graham Stanton suggests "revelatory moments." These scenes are indeed just that—revelatory moments. And they are also apocalyptic moments for those who experienced them. Persons who experienced the first Easter revelatory moments wrote nothing. What we have in the Gospels is a faint echo of those moments. They cannot be dismissed as "myths and legends." They are something else. Certainly they are not to be read as full-fledged accounts, as one would write up an incident for a newspaper. Indeed, a newspaper article is never a complete and literal record of all the writer is reporting. But neither is he or she reporting a myth or legend. The amazing thing is that the witness of those who experienced the first revelatory or apocalyptic moments has come to us with such simple yet powerful clarity. Ernst Käsemann, *New Testament Questions of Today* (London: SCM, 1969), believes that "apocalyptic themes" formed "the real beginning of primitive Christian theology." If so, then the appearance scenes here and elsewhere in the Gospels would be revelatory experiences understood in an apocalyptic sense. The abbreviated scenes that have come to us in the Gospels are less descriptive and more indicative of the power of God. Pheme Perkins rightly expresses a need to "recover a way into the reality of that earlier world of discourse." That need makes it difficult to interpret the appearance scenes. *See Resurrection, New Testament Witness, and Contemporary Reflection* (Garden City NY: Doubleday & Co., 1984).

[2]The doctrine of the Trinity was not officially formulated until much later, yet Matthew's Gospel contains a clear affirmation of it. If it was added later, then there is no problem. If not, what can we say? I suggest that, without formulating any official doctrine, the first believers found they were experiencing God in three ways: as Father (God) as Holy Spirit (as in the Hebrew Scriptures and as Christians had experienced), and as "Son" (Jesus). The official baptismal formula may have been added later, but the concept of God in three persons was perhaps a gradual realization that needed no official formulation. Matthew's Gospel puts it into words and couples its authority and power with the Great Commission.

[3]"The Son of Man coming" refers to a harvest, and other images point to an end. No details are given. It is the apocalyptic way simply to declare victory at the end, nothing more except to declare that

good will triumph and evil will perish. It can be understood as some present good doing battle against some present evil, which will be defeated, and not necessarily referring to the end of everything.

[4]"Then" and "now" are ways of saying that "then" can be either in time or beyond time. "Now" is whatever present struggle with evil threatens. "Now," even in the struggle, the victory is assured "then."

[5]Apocalyptic faith requires that "time" be removed from our faith-thinking. A close look at the sayings of Jesus concerning the end shows that he was careful not to define times and seasons.

CHAPTER 5

THE ACT OF GOD IN LUKE-ACTS

In the Gospels Jesus does not appear by chance. He does not speak in his name. He does not raise himself from the dead. What he is, what he says, what he does, and what happens to him assume the greatest significance. Nevertheless, it is all for one reason: God is the prime mover, and Jesus is the act of God. This means that in Jesus the power and faithfulness of God are at stake. Jesus is not at stake; God is. It is all well and good to speak of a "Christ-centered" faith. Christian faith is Christ-centered, but first it has to be God-centered. In Luke's Gospel and the book of Acts, Jesus and his resurrection are firmly portrayed as the acts of God.

The Witness of the Angels

Apocalyptic writing makes much use of angels as God's messengers, announcing what God is doing and why. In the beginning of Luke's Gospel angels are everywhere.[1] "An angel of the Lord" stands on "the right side of the altar of incense" (1:11) and announces to Zechariah that his son will be the forerunner of Jesus as the Messiah. "The angel Gabriel was sent by God to a town in Galilee called Nazareth, to a virgin engaged to a man whose name was Joseph" (1:26-27). The angel announces to Mary that she will have a son sent from God. Mary's song (1:46-55) extols what God intends to do:

scatter the proud, bring down the powerful from their thrones, lift up the lowly, fill the hungry. The victory of God is promised "to give light to those who sit in darkness and in the shadow of death" (1:79). The angel of the Lord announces to shepherds "good news of great joy," and is joined by a "multitude of the heavenly host" (2:8-13). All these angels have but one function, and that is to announce the action and purpose of God in Jesus. Christmas points to the action and purpose of God in Jesus, which culminates in the resurrection. Zechariah, Mary, and the shepherds point to what God is doing in the child that is being born.

"This Is My Son" (9:35)

Moreover, God is the primary witness in Luke. At the baptism of Jesus there is a voice from heaven, saying, "You are my Son, the Beloved" (3:21-22). In the transfiguration scene Moses and Elijah appear with Jesus on the mountain in the presence of Peter, James, and John. Moses and Elijah may represent the Law and the Prophets attesting to Jesus, but there is a higher voice, proclaiming, "This is my Son, my Chosen."

When the Son begins to preach, he calls for faithfulness. When the owner of the home comes, stewards are to be found living in faith, their manner of life attesting to this faith. He sees "Satan fall from heaven like a flash of lightning" (10:18). That is, in apocalyptic language, he sees the defeat of evil and the victory of God even in the success of the seventy whom he has sent, something that is at once both "now" and "then." Satan fallen has both temporal and cosmic significance. Simply put, it is apocalyptic language for the defeat of evil.

Jesus' call for faithfulness is issued in this light. He calls stewards to be faithful and wise. This means that a faith-decision and a lifestyle choice are required (12:49-51). He calls this decision and choice striving to enter by "the narrow door," and says that "some are last who will be first, and some are first who will be last" (13:30). He uses the figure of a homeowner who returns from a journey and shuts the door. Those outside are the faithless who did not conduct their lives believing in the victory of God's kingdom-rule. The faithful, on the other hand, will come "from east and west, from north and south, and will eat in the kingdom of God" with Abraham, Isaac, Jacob, and all the prophets (13:28-29). In announcing the defeat of evil and the coming victory of God, Jesus places himself on the side of apocalyptic faith.

"The Days Are Coming" (17:22)

Jesus teaches that the final crisis, a time undefined, will demand faithfulness. At the same time, and perhaps more importantly, he declares that the kingdom-rule of God is in their midst. That is, God's sovereign rule is present and calls for response. There will be times when that rule is asserted in the future, and there will also be an end when that rule is finally asserted.

The end is described in apocalyptic language: "For as the lightning flashes and lights up the sky from one side to the other, so will the Son of Man be in his day" (17:24). The days before the end will be characterized by unfaithfulness *and* faithfulness "as it was in days of Noah and Lot" (17:26, 28). But the faithful are called to remain faithful: "Those who try to make their life secure will lose it, but those who lose their life will keep it" (17:33). As to where and when the end will be, there is a cryptic answer: "Where the corpse is, there the vultures will gather" (17:37). The end comes when the time is right, a moment only God can know. There is no attempt to say where or when. Jesus simply affirms the end and the certainty of the victory of God and the Son of man, while urging faithfulness upon those who believe.

The theme of faithful endurance continues. The days will come when the Temple will be destroyed. But even in such a time the faithful are not to say "the time is near" (21:8). In the face of "wars and insurrections" they are not to be afraid, "but the end will not follow immediately" (21:9). There is a description of the future in apocalyptic language: "Nation will rise against nation . . . there will be great earthquakes, and in various places famines and plagues; and there will be dreadful portents and great signs from heaven" (21:10-11). This is the stuff of history.

The faithful are to be concerned only about their testimony. They are not to fear death. Only faithful endurance is required: "By your endurance you will gain your souls" (21:19). When there are upheavals in nations and among nations, even when Jerusalem is surrounded by armies (21:20), they are to remain faithful, believing in God's power and eventual victory. Toward the latter part of the first century this would have special meaning for believers. The second coming is delayed. Time stretches forward with no sign of the final triumph. In the meantime, faithfulness is to be their watchword. At the end of the twentieth century and the beginning of the twenty-first, it remains more than ever the watchword.

When the exhortation to faithfulness extends to the end, the language becomes decidedly apocalyptic: "signs in the sun, the moon, and the stars, and on the earth distress among nations confused by the roaring of the sea and the waves. People will faint from fear and foreboding of what is coming upon the world, for the powers of the heavens will be shaken" (21:25-26). None of this is to be taken literally or to be looked for literally. This is typical apocalyptic language to describe the consummate victory of God.

At that victory "they will see the Son of Man coming in a cloud with power and great glory" (21:27). The coming "in a cloud with power and great glory" reflects the picture in Daniel 7 when one "like a human being" comes with "the clouds of heaven" and is given "dominion and glory and kingship" (vv. 13-14). This can be a picture either of the triumph of the Messiah or of the triumph of the Messiah with the people of

God at the end. The faithful are called to stand firm in that faith: "Now when these things begin to take place, stand up and raise your heads, because your redemption is drawing near" (21:28). Those who live in faith see this redemption always drawing near. They are to raise their heads against whatever storm, not in fear but in hope.

"Two Men in Dazzling Clothes" (24:4)

What is it that underscores the peril of faithlessness and the hope of redemption? It is the empty tomb. Mark has a "young man dressed in a white robe" sitting before the empty tomb. In Matthew, an angel is sitting on the stone. Now in Luke there are "two men . . . in dazzling clothes." Present, according to Luke, are "the women who had come with him from Galilee" (23:55). They are identified as "Mary Magdalene, Joanna, Mary the mother of James, and the other women with them" (24:10). Luke sees them "perplexed" and "terrified" at the empty tomb. What is this scene intended to mean?

"Two men in dazzling clothes" appear to tell them what it means. The two men, along with Matthew's angel sitting on the stone and Mark's "young man dressed in a white robe," are apocalyptic messengers. They announce that Jesus is "living"; he is no longer "among the dead" (24:5). It is worth noting here the following comment from the *Interpreter's Dictionary of the Bible*:

> Like all ancient peoples, the Hebrews believed that the dead, though they relinquished the earthly scene, did not relinquish existence per se. Somewhere in a region outside the earth but accessible to God (Job 26:6; Ps 139:8; Amos 9:2), they lingered on, oblivious of their former lives . . . bereft of all mundane pleasures, freed at last from the "sick fatigue" of the flesh . . . yet at the same time divorced from empirical experience of God's presence . . . and hence with nothing for which to thank or praise him.[2]

The place of the dead is called "Sheol," or "Hades." But the two men declare that Jesus is not "among the dead," that is, not in the abode of the dead. He is not dead, and he is not "among the dead." He is living. The later Christian creeds would say that he is "sitting at the right hand of God." In other words, Jesus has been exalted by God. His life has not been allowed to fall to the ground. This underscores the affirmation of final victory and the call to the faith choice that leads to the open or shut door. Jesus may not be sought "among the dead."

"Was It Not Necessary?" (24:26)

When brought to the understanding that Jesus is living and his death was not a tragic defeat, the first community had to understand his death. The "two men in dazzling clothes" have another message for the women: "Remember how he told you, while he was still in Galilee, that the Son of Man must be handed over to sinners, and be crucified, and on the third day rise again" (24:6). The emphasis of the early witness, according to Luke, was on the word "must." The theme of the necessity of his death is carried further in the story that follows the women at the tomb—the encounter between a stranger and two disciples on the road to Emmaus.

Emmaus has never been definitely identified, but it does not matter. What matters are the two points Luke emphasizes in this story: what Jesus teaches and how he is recognized. Jesus joins them on the way, but he is not known to them. They are discussing the recent tragic death of Jesus, whom they had expected to be the Messiah, the one who would "restore the kingdom to Israel" (Acts 1:6). The death of the Messiah is certainly not to be considered. The entire discussion between the stranger and the two disciples concerns one thing—the necessity of the death of the Messiah. Jesus asks, "Was it not necessary that the Messiah should suffer these things and then enter into his glory?" Then, beginning with "Moses and all the prophets," Jesus interprets to them the things about himself found in the scriptures (24:26-27).

After Jesus' death the Gospel writers show the early community believing that the Hebrew Scriptures speak of the necessity of a suffering messiah. Later Christian believers have read Isaiah 53, for example, with eyes looking at the cross and empty tomb. Acts 8:26 and 1 Peter 2:22 and following are also cited. Christian believers came to believe in a suffering yet triumphant servant of the Lord. Jesus must "enter into his glory" by way of suffering and death. There was no problem with the seeming contradiction of triumph through suffering and death; just as Ezekiel saw triumph coming out of the suffering of the exiles, and all by the act of God.

In this story Luke also emphasizes a unique way by which the exalted Jesus is recognized. At the end of the journey there is a meal with the stranger. According to the story, the two recognized him when "he took bread, blessed and broke it" (24:30-31). The blessing and breaking of the bread are familiar to Luke and his readers. Even though Christ vanishes from sight when they return to the world, when they return to the Table, they find their hearts "burning within" with his presence.

"Thought They Were Seeing a Ghost" (24:37)

Luke joins the story on the Emmaus Road with the disciples in the Upper Room. The two disciples return to Jerusalem and report their experience. Immediately, according to Luke, Jesus stands among them, but they are "startled and terrified" and think they are "seeing a ghost" (24:36). Jesus invites them to view his hands and feet. There is the suggestion of a body, but also a spirit. Luke's purpose is not to help us visualize this. Rather, he wants us to understand that the first community experienced the Jesus whom they had known as living, exalted by God.[3]

In this scene much attention is given to the necessity of the death of Jesus. The "two men in dazzling clothes" reminded the women of its necessity. The two disciples on the Emmaus road were also reminded of its necessity. Here in the upper room the disciples are reminded of its necessity. Jesus reminds them of his words while he is still with them, "that everything written about me in the law of Moses, the prophets, and the psalms must be fulfilled" (24:44). Luke notes a period of instruction: "Then he opened their minds to understand the scriptures, and he said to them, 'Thus it is written, that the Messiah is to suffer and to rise from the dead on the third day, and that repentance and forgiveness of sins is to be proclaimed in his name to all nations, beginning from Jerusalem'" (24:45-47).[4]

This sounds much like a formal affirmation of the later Christian understanding of Jesus and the scriptures. Certainly by the latter part of the first century, Christians were reading the Hebrew Scriptures in this way, believing that the early community had received the commission "that repentance and forgiveness of sins is to be proclaimed in his name to all nations, beginning from Jerusalem." Whatever the experience in the upper room may have been, the suffering and dead Jesus whom they had known in life has been raised according to the will and purpose of God. Roman crucifixion was the great horror, a sign of Roman triumph. But the Christians of the first century seem never to have been embarrassed by the cross of Jesus. On the contrary, they witnessed to it as both a necessity and a triumph.[5] Something has been done to the "No" of the cross.

"Two Men in White Robes" (Acts 1:10)

Luke closes his Gospel with the promise of the coming of the power of the Holy Spirit. Jesus parts from the disciples with a blessing; and the first community returns joyfully "blessing God." Luke's second volume, the book of Acts, opens with

Jesus' forty days on earth. He "presented himself alive to [the apostles] by many convincing proofs, appearing to them during forty days and speaking about the kingdom of God" (1:3). What does this mean?

It emphasizes what Luke has already presented in his Gospel. The first community became convinced that Jesus was living, but Luke does not give any details here of their experiences. The forty days are not mentioned by any of the other Gospel writers. "Forty days" refers to an indefinite period of time following the death of Jesus, similar to the forty years of wilderness wanderings by the Israelites. It definitely indicates a period of time following the death of Jesus when the first community had experiences that induced their faith without question that Jesus had been raised by God. It may also suggest that the first community of faith reached this level of faith over a longer period of time than we might suppose from the Gospel records.

During this time the disciples ask if Jesus will "restore the kingdom to Israel" (1:6). That is, will the promise of Ezekiel and the other prophets for the return and restoration of Israel be fulfilled literally in an earthly Jewish kingdom?[5] Instead of answering the question directly, Jesus tells them that they are not "to know the times or periods that the Father has set by his own authority" (v. 7). He turns immediately to the commission suggested in the closing verses of Luke's Gospel: "You will be my witnesses in Jerusalem and in all Judea and Samaria, and to the ends of the earth" (v. 8). Then he is lifted up, and a cloud takes him out of their sight (v. 9).

Without taking this literally, its truth can still be understood as affirming the physical removal of Jesus from this earth. Immediately, "two men in white robes stood by them" (v. 10). Apocalyptic messengers arrive again to make their announcement: "This Jesus, who was been taken up from you into heaven, will come in the same way as you saw him go into heaven" (v. 11b). This is essentially the same announcement that was made earlier in Luke's Gospel. There will be an end, with the return of Jesus as the triumphant Son of Man. The future victory is assured. In the meantime, the messengers have a commission to witness "to the end of the earth." "Times and periods" are in the Father's "authority."

Focusing too much attention on details concerning the going and return of Jesus may result in missing what Luke urges: faithfulness in witnessing to what God has done in Jesus. In Acts 2:24 and following, after the Pentecostal experience, Peter preaches a sermon. He declares that what is happening is really the fulfillment of the prophet Joel, who spoke of God "in the last days" pouring out the Spirit upon all flesh (Joel 2:28-32; Acts 2:17-21). According to Joel, God's victory is to be shown "in the last days." This victory is spoken of in apocalyptic terms: "I will show portents in the heavens and on the earth, blood and fire and columns of smoke. The sun shall be turned to darkness, and the moon to blood, before the great and terrible day the Lord comes" (Joel 2: 30-31).

What actually happened? Certainly nothing as literal or as limited as the sun turned to darkness or the moon to blood. Rather, Jesus of Nazareth has been "crucified and killed by the hands of those outside the law . . . God raised . . . up, having freed him from death, because it was impossible for him to be held in its power" (Acts 2:23). Psalm 16 is quoted as affirming that God's "Holy One" will not be allowed to see corruption (vv. 26-28). Jesus, as God's Holy One, has not been abandoned to the dark abode of the dead. He is not "among the dead," as the "two men in dazzling clothes" had told the women at the tomb: "God raised him up." In the light of the faithfulness of God, the people are called to turn (repent) and respond to God's kingdom/rule: "Repent, and be baptized every one of you in the name of Jesus Christ so that your sins may be forgiven; and you will receive the gift of the Holy Spirit" (v. 38). But none of this matters, unless God has raised him from the dead.

The Meaning for Faith

I said in the beginning of this chapter that the stakes are high, because God is placed on the line. If God is helpless in the face of Jesus on the cross, then where is the kingdom-rule? There is no rule, no sovereignty of good over evil. Ezekiel and Daniel were wrong. The first Easter experience was strong enough to launch a faith that believed there is a rule, a sovereignty of good over evil because Jesus was the act of God. This is where the preacher stands and Christian witness begins. Before the preacher's mouth is opened to speak, before the sermon notes are prepared, before the call to worship, this faith waits to be preached, together with a call to turn and make a faith-choice that casts life on the side of the angels.

What does all this mean for faith? I have to say that the witness of the first community through Luke (and the other Gospel writers) is so powerful that I, who never saw the empty tomb or the upper room, am moved to cast my life on the side of God. I am moved to do this in the face of the evil that did not perish with Rome and that is still capable of inflicting great pain and destruction. Evil and its pain may be necessary, as it was with Jesus. But the message of the scene in the upper room contains the essence of the faith that calls us to courage and hope until the end. The message is that God is faithful, Jesus is raised, and God may be trusted to the end. This kind of faith is in the language and spirit of apocalyptic faith. The affirmation behind the upper room scene is apocalyptic and eschatological. It affirms the victory both now and at the end. The proof of the scene is in the power it has to call forth faith-choices and lifestyle decisions, along with the hope it gives in the God who raises the dead.

The Jesus of Easter should be seen as a strange and startling sight indeed. He can raise more questions than answers. Believers are not instantly made by rushing them into his presence, even if the preacher assures them that this means they will live forever. Many never return to church until Christmas.

The risen Jesus provokes questioning, and even worry. The empty tomb is not a place of great comfort. Both preacher and people might do well to be startled and troubled. Easter, like the ancient "day of the Lord" in the Old Testament, is not necessarily a day of light. As in the prophet Amos:

> Alas for you who desire the day of the Lord! Why do you want the day of the Lord? It is darkness, not light; as if someone fled from a lion, and was met by a bear. (5:18)

With the empty tomb and the exalted Jesus, evil in any form now stands stripped of its invincibility. Justice rises and calls out for followers, and a great light gleams from its sword.

The scene at supper in Emmaus needs to be recast around the Communion Table. When we celebrate the sacrament, the exalted Jesus is proclaimed. We have never been to the upper room or empty tomb, but we can be taken there through preaching the resurrection and in the breaking of the bread. At times other than Easter, the Communion service can have greater power and meaning by linking it with the resurrection, and especially the apocalyptic faith of the resurrection. We find ourselves in the presence of the exalted Christ who intercedes for us. He may join us on some Emmaus Road.

At the same time that the apocalyptic message of the resurrection of Jesus and the final triumph of God are raised, emphasis should be placed on the message and the mission, not details concerning the end. The message of Luke-Acts is that Jesus has been raised and withdrawn from the community by the act of God. The withdrawal of the bodily Jesus is to be replaced by the power of the Holy Spirit. Disciples are to remain faithful and to witness to God's victory at the cross now, as well as to the final victory. The end and the time of the end remain in God's hands. Dwelling upon the victory at the end neglects the more important faith that the victory is both now and then.

The church in the latter part of the first century felt it had a commission to witness "to the ends of the earth." This commission remains. Why not rediscover and reexamine the commission as a witness to the victory of God over evil? It is a faith we proclaim, not a religion. Preaching Jesus as exalted by God is preaching the act of God in defeating evil. In this witness, repentance, forgiveness, and the love of God may be proclaimed without denigrating any religion. (After all, Christianity began as a faith, not a religion.) Witnessing to the love of God in schools and hospitals or fighting for human rights may be done as witness to the sovereign love of God, not to condemn the world, but that the world might be saved. Saved from what? Saved from yielding to the defeat of sin, from prejudice and injustice, from hunger, from other faith-commitments and lifestyle choices that deny God's love and sovereignty and that end in death. Certainly there are religions that do not acknowledge a personal God, or a God at all—to say nothing of believing in a life to come. Nevertheless, the apocalyptic faith of the risen Jesus and the great commission call for witness to the good news that God is, God loves the world, and evil does not have the last word.

Notes

[1]D. S. Russell, *Divine Disclosure: An Introduction to Jewish Apocalyptic* (Minneapolis: Fortress Press, 1992) 77, notes that "angels are divine messengers who shuttle back and forth between heaven and earth. . . . But more common . . . is their function as celestial guides or celestial interpreters."

[2]"Abode of the Dead," in *The Interpreter's Bible*, vol. 1 (New York /Nashville: Abingdon, 1962) 787.

[3]The appearance scenes have been dismissed as myths and legends, but they came from somewhere and were incorporated into the Gospels. No one has suggested that the Gospel writers made them up. From whence, then, did they come if not from the oral tradition of eyewitnesses and ministers of the word? Some would object to the idea of a fabrication. The exact nature of those appearances may be

lost to us, but not the fact. But they do suggest that the early Easter communities witnessed an experience of the exalted Jesus in apocalyptic terms that God had indeed prevailed.

[4]"Thus it is written" reflects the early church reading of the Hebrew Scriptures. In the latter part of the first century the church believed the Hebrew Scriptures pointed to the suffering Christ and began to cite passages such as Isaiah 53. For example, 1 Peter 3:18 reflects the understanding of Jesus as the Suffering Servant, an example to other suffering Christians.

[5]The Jewish-Christian conflict in the first century, particularly in the latter part, is highlighted if not exacerbated by the Christian reading of the Old Testament or Hebrew Scriptures. Christians saw themselves as the "new Israel" (see 1 Pet 2:1-9; compare with the language in Exod 19:1-6).

CHAPTER 6

LIGHT AGAINST DARKNESS IN JOHN

The Gospel of John was written during the final decade of the first century or early in the second century. Although other Gospels were written around this time, only the Gospel of John survived to be placed with Matthew, Mark, and Luke. Tradition assigns authorship to the apostle John. His Gospel represents an understanding of Jesus that had emerged in his community. Therefore, John is quite different from the other three. For example, the language is different. Jesus says plainly who he is. There are long discourses by Jesus. In short, the entire Gospel is concerned with telling what Jesus means: "These are written so that you may come to believe that Jesus is the Messiah, the Son of God" (20:31). The fact that John's Gospel was preserved suggests that he succeeded in his purpose. This chapter is concerned with John's understanding of the meaning of the risen Jesus.

"The Light Shines in the Darkness" (1:5)

The prologue (1:1-18) is a strong affirmation of faith. It declares that Jesus coexisted with God "in the beginning" as the Word that made all things. Jesus is called the "light" that "shines in the darkness, and the darkness did not overcome it" (1:5). In apocalyptic thought, light and darkness represent the battle between good and evil. For the Jews, it is God and their enemies. For the Christians, it is evil against the exalted Christ of God. In the book of Revelation it is the dragon (evil) against the rider on the white horse (the exalted Christ), who is then followed by the armies of heaven (19:11-16). Which will win—good or evil? Or will both be locked in a never-ending conflict?

"The darkness did not overcome it." John and the Christians of his time knew the darkness well. They lived with corruption, persecution, slavery, the oppression of women, and a declining empire. Soon after the prologue, John the Baptist announces: "Here is the Lamb of God who takes away the sin of the world" (1:29). His announcement is more than the assurance of pardon following the formal confession of sin in a worship service. It has to do with the defeat of darkness. In John 1:51 Jesus declares to Nathanael that he "will see heaven opened and the angels of God ascending and descending upon the Son of Man." This is apocalyptic language. It is in the context of the light overcoming the darkness, God being "known" in the Son, and Jesus hailed as the Lamb of God who takes away the sin of the world.[1]

"The Resurrection and the Life" (11:28)

In John's Gospel the war of good and evil is light versus darkness and perishing versus eternal life. All who believe will "not perish but may have eternal life" (3:16). In chapter 10 Jesus says: "My sheep hear my voice. I know them, and they follow me. I give them eternal life, and they will never perish." (vv. 27-28). Prior to this, Jesus declared himself to be "the light of the world" (8:12). The climax of this assurance is in Jesus' words to Martha after the raising of Lazarus: "I am the resurrection and the life. Those who believe in me, even though they die, will live, and everyone who lives and believes in me will never die" (11:25-26).

The issue is faith: "Those who believe in me." Without seeing the resurrected Christ, John and his readers must believe in him and in God who has not abandoned him: "My sheep hear my voice . . . and they will never perish . . . Those who believe in me . . . will never die." "Believe in God, believe also in me" (14:1). So John hears Jesus issuing a strong call to faith: "Walk while you have the light, so that the darkness may not overtake you. . . . While you have the light, believe in the light, so that you may become children of light" (12:35-36). The call to faith is to believe that Jesus is "lifted up," that God has defeated the power of death and the evil that crucified Jesus. "The ruler of this world will be driven out" (12:31). That is, whoever or whatever is leading the battle against God and the people of faith is defeated.

"I Have Seen the Lord" (20:18)

Throughout John's Gospel belief in God's victory through Jesus is crucial. Jesus is the Word become flesh. He is the light that darkness cannot overcome. He is the Lamb of God who "takes away the sin of the world." He is the Shepherd whose voice must be heeded. Whoever believes in him will not "perish." In short, throughout his Gospel, John declares that something final has been done in Jesus. As in the other Gospels, however, it is only after the death of Jesus that the disciples understand.

John says that after the entry into Jerusalem on Palm Sunday, "His disciples did not understand these things at first; but when Jesus was glorified, then they remembered that these things had been written of him and had been done to him" (12:16). What had been "written" was the promise of Zechariah: "Do not be afraid, daughter of Zion. Look, your king is coming, sitting on a donkey's colt" (12:15). Only after Jesus' death did the disciples come to believe that God had exalted him. They opposed his going to Jerusalem. They deserted him in the final hours. They did not see in him the messiah who would "restore the kingdom to Israel" (Acts 1:6). No one was found at the cross rubbing their hands, as it were, and declaring that death and evil were being conquered. Afterward they are portrayed as people who took to the streets and risked their lives to proclaim Jesus as Messiah and savior.

John also traces this change to what happened following the crucifixion. All that John has been saying about the victorious "light" comes to a focus in the resurrection scenes following the death of Jesus, in particular Mary Magdalene's encounter at the empty tomb and the disciples in the upper room. Added by a later hand, there is also the scene by the sea when Peter was restored. Mary Magdalene comes first to the tomb while it is still dark and sees that the stone is taken away from the tomb (20:1). She runs to report to Peter and John that "they have taken the Lord out of the tomb, and we do not know where they have laid him" (20:2). This is a straightforward and down-to-earth account. Because the tomb is empty, we assume the body has been removed. There is no announcement of the resurrection, simply that the tomb is found empty.

The narrative continues. Peter and the "other disciple," presumably John, come to see for themselves. They see the linen clothes and napkin that had been on his head "rolled up in a place by itself" (20:4-7), which is, in itself, an interesting bit of specific detail. A significant statement is made concerning the other disciple: "Then the other disciple, who reached the tomb first, also went in, *and he saw and believed* (20:8, italics mine). What did he see? Linen cloths, the napkin, and the empty tomb. In other words, the other disciple believed on the basis of seeing the tomb empty.[2] John 20:9 then makes this comment: "For as yet they did not understand the scripture, that he must rise from the dead." What scripture? It is not given. Certainly by the late first century, Christians had come to read the Hebrew Scriptures as affirming the death and resurrection of Jesus. But at this point the other disciple does not have to know that. Here he believes after seeing the empty tomb. According to John, therefore, the earliest Easter experience was an empty tomb, and belief accompanied that experience.

Now the scene, together with the language and imagery, abruptly shifts. Mary Magdalene is seen standing and weeping outside the tomb (20:11). No one else is present. She looks into the tomb and sees "two angels in white, sitting where the body of Jesus had been lying, one at the head and the other at the feet" (20:12). Where were the angels when Peter and the other disciple were there? The introduction of angels is important. Whereas in apocalyptic writing angels usually announce something God has done or will do, here they make no announcement, but in apocalyptic fashion their presence indicates something important concerning the empty tomb. They stand with Mark's "young man dressed in a white robe" and Matthew's angel.

Immediately Mary encounters Jesus. A formal exchange follows between them. Jesus speaks her name, and she calls him "Teacher," but the words of Jesus suggest something more. He forbids her to touch him, saying, "I have not yet ascended to the Father. But go to the brothers and say to them, 'I am ascending to my Father and your Father, to my God and your God' " (20:17). Here Jesus identifies himself to Mary as being exalted by God. Moreover, this exaltation by God is by the same God in whom they believe. The word of Jesus to Mary is that the God who has raised him up is "my Father and your Father . . . my God and your God." The message is that the God of their faith is indeed faithful. Jesus has not been abandoned.

Earlier in this chapter we noted the promise of Jesus to Nathanael that he would "see heaven opened and the angels of God ascending and descending upon the Son of Man." This is apocalyptic imagery referring to the triumph of God and the victory of God's faithful people. It recalls the picture in Daniel 7:9-14. In Daniel's picture God is on the throne. God's enemies are destroyed, and "one like a human being" is "presented before him" and is given "dominion and glory and kingship."

The victory of faith is promised through the sovereignty of a faithful God. This is the message given in the scene with Mary and Jesus.

The formal scene between Mary and Jesus and the angels concludes with Mary going to the disciples, announcing, "I have seen the Lord" (20:18). The word for "see" can also have a metaphorical meaning to indicate a seeing beyond mere sensual seeing, a seeing to perceive or understand.[3] In the next chapter we will see the encounter with the exalted Christ that John of Patmos describes in Revelation 1. He uses apocalyptic language to affirm the risen and exalted Jesus seen through the eyes of faith and by the power of the Holy Spirit. So Mary's announcement needs to be expanded beyond a physical seeing. It indicates an understanding of those who participated in the first Easter experience that is beyond the physical. It is to be heard as a declaration of the victory of God, the victory of light over darkness.

"We Have Seen the Lord" (20:25)

John continues with the scene in the upper room. Matthew and Luke write of the experience in the upper room, but John gives it the touch of an artist, and even perhaps a poet. The disciples are found in the upper room on "the first day of the week." The day in the upper room had in all probability become important for Christian worship by John's time. "Jesus came and stood among them" (20:19). He offers his "shalom" (peace) and shows them his hands and his side. He commissions them: "As the Father has sent me, so I send you" (20:21b). Pentecost happens instantly. He "breathes" on them and gives them the Holy Spirit. They receive formal authority to "forgive" or "retain" sins. Then the scene ends abruptly. It is more of a résumé than a connected narrative: disciples experience the risen Christ and receive a commission and the power of the Holy Spirit.

Thomas is now added to the scene in the upper room. When he enters a week later, the other disciples tell him: "We have seen the Lord" (20:25), echoing Mary's previous announcement. He, too, experiences the risen Jesus as the same Jesus whom he had known before death, but now with the wounds of death. Thomas acknowledges Jesus as "My Lord and my God" (20:28). He now stands with the other disciples in the upper room with the risen Christ and participates in the commission and power of the Holy Spirit. Thomas is invited to touch the wounds of Jesus. John leaves no doubt that the disciples experienced the same Jesus after death as they had known before death.

How Are We To Believe?

"These are written so that you may come to believe" (20:31). What is John's Gospel asking the disciples, or us, to believe? What would believers at the end of the first century (or at the beginning of the twentieth-first) be expected to believe? They have not seen Jesus either before or after his death. Yet they believe, or are asked to believe. Believe what? Surely not just that Thomas finally believed, or even that Jesus appeared and reappeared behind closed doors. They are asked to believe much more. They are asked to believe that Jesus of Nazareth, crucified under Pontius Pilate, has been exalted by God. The love and compassion he showed, the forgiveness he grants, the entrance into the kingdom of God he gave—all these were not defeated by the evil that killed him. Rather, the opposite is true. A decisive battle has been fought and evil's destruction assured. This is the witness that comes from these scenes in John's Gospel. "These are written so that you may come to believe that Jesus is the Messiah, the Son of God, and that through believing you may have life in his name" (20:31).

These scenes in John's Gospel express the same message as those in the Gospels of Matthew and Luke: something happened to the first Easter community that brought them to a pronounced faith powerful enough to energize defeated and hopeless people. John describes their witness in scenes whose very simplicity can be deceiving. The encounter with Mary Magdalene, the two scenes in the upper room, and even the one by the sea must be read for what lies behind them—the faith that light has not been overcome by darkness. Mary's announcement "I have seen the Lord" and the disciples' affirmation "We have seen the Lord" are beyond the metaphorical and cannot be adequately explained as mythological. Like the Apostles Creed (or any other creed), they suggest far more than they can say. Like poetry, they express a truth that can be lost if analyzed too closely. I believe these scenes should be viewed in that light. I hope that those who cannot read them literally will not abandon them and thus miss the faith they are intended to convey. I also hope that those who do read them literally will not miss the larger faith they are intended to convey.

One colleague, after reading the preceding pages, spoke of the faith-experience of Mary Magdalene and the disciples as an apocalyptic moment. I think his point is well taken. I can see these scenes portraying apocalyptic moments, a breaking in of the truth of the victory of God, though not expressed in apocalyptic language. Certainly these are revelatory moments, as Graham Stanton once suggested to me. They are moments when faith and hope are revived. These scenes in John's Gospel and in the other Gospels do not tell us exactly what happened. John gives us revelatory moments. Who among second-generation Christians can describe exactly the revelatory moment or moments when faith is kindled or revived? Even on Easter, with the great hymns and affirmations, how would we describe our faith? When all is said and done, we leave our great moments of worship with the faith that God is to be trusted in life and beyond life. But can we put it precisely into words? And what about those moments in addition to Easter, those moments when the darkness descends and threatens what little light we have? Then faith and hope revive. Jesus appears again in that upper room of fear. Are they not also revelatory moments that translate into an apocalyptic faith and hope that the present darkness will not prevail?

I believe those in the first community had their moments, but their witness has come to us through the Gospels in pictures that point to an experience that is beyond words, but not beyond the heart. The poet will not analyze or define a sunset, knowing that in analysis beauty can be lost. The poet tries to help us experience the beauty with words that free us to seek truth, but do not bind. So these resurrection scenes in the Gospels attempt to lead us toward the beauty. This is also the work of the preacher who attempts to preach the resurrection.

"Blessed are those who believe" that God has exalted Jesus and live believing this is so. They are blessed, not because they get higher marks than Thomas, but because they can live with meaning and empowerment. There is an overcoming within the darkness. They do not perish, even though the struggle may be long and there is no immediate victory. The Holy Spirit is breathed upon this faith, which becomes mission.

I think of the long years past and still to come when faith must wait upon captive hostages and other victims of injustice, greed, the desire for power, and the many assorted evils that have inflicted their pain upon this world. But faith shall overcome—faith that God has exalted Jesus, faith that I shall not perish in this present darkness. I am reminded of the song "We Shall Overcome," which was first sung by Christians in slave cabins. Its original words are based upon the same faith John affirms in his Gospel: "The light shines in the darkness, and the darkness did not overcome it" (1:5).

History books tell of John's time and will also tell of our time. What affirmation of faith is strong enough to challenge despair and cynicism? What about the darkness through which we live? I recall President Bush speaking at the fiftieth anniversary of the bombing of Pearl Harbor of "summoning light against the dark." I believe he was quoting President Eisenhower. I thought of John's affirmation about the light not being overcome by the darkness. For believers in the first century, the battle was joined, and the issue was not in doubt. "The darkness did not overcome it." It is like a single candle in a dark room. John's Gospel summons light against the darkness. The light must be cast against whatever "darkness" threatens to overcome us—hate attempting to overcome love, prejudice attempting to overcome compassion, the lust for power among people and nations attempting to overcome the search for the common good for all people.

In John's Gospel the risen Jesus gives "fullness" and "grace upon grace." He comes to his own home, but is rejected. "But to all who received him, who believed in his name, he gave power to become children of God" (1:12). The risen Jesus gives us power to love, to show compassion, and to forgive. These are the marks of the "children of God." Hate, prejudice, and an unforgiving spirit are the products of darkness. "The darkness did not overcome it." These words must be cast against the darkness, not only to condemn the darkness, but also to recover the faith that the darkness will not overcome. This is the larger work to which faith is called.

Believing (and preaching) the resurrection is standing upon a perilous boundary between perishing and having eternal life. Morality, justice, hope, and courage in the face of our human ills and problems—all these call for faith that God did not abandon Jesus and can be trusted—by anyone—to the end. We "sheep" are always waiting to hear that voice.

We hear the voice of the Shepherd gladly. "As the Father has sent me, so I send you" (20:21b). The words "so I send you" call for the deepest and most serious consideration. It is a commission to live faithfully unto death, bearing even the silence of God. It is to be sent out as "lambs among wolves," to love in the face of hate, to be servants not masters. Like the apostles, we receive the Holy Spirit, for we know we need that power. We receive it with trembling, for the Holy Spirit is not given so that we do no more than sing gladly in the springtime.

"Blessed are those who have not seen and yet have come to believe" (20:29b). They might deserve higher marks than

Thomas or the other disciples. Thomas and his doubts are incidental to this declaration. This is a word for John and his second-generation believers, or would-be believers, who had not seen the empty tomb or participated in the Easter experience.

To believe, must we have literal visions of the risen Jesus? According to the Gospel writers, only a few people actually saw the risen Jesus. Since the resurrection, vast numbers have had to find their faith by means other than being in the upper room or hearing angelic announcements outside the empty tomb. No preacher can or should make any secret of that, for he or she stands in the number who rely upon the witness of the Holy Spirit. These scenes in John and the other Gospels speak their message, but it is the Holy Spirit who brings the faith that God has exalted Jesus.

There is scholarly agreement that John's Gospel ends with chapter 20 and that chapter 21 was added by a later hand. It is a scene familiar to many through sermons on Jesus forgiving and commissioning Peter. Here Jesus is revealed to Peter and a group of disciples, including Nathanael, Thomas, James and John. The person who added this chapter probably sought to restore Peter into good graces or to show the disciples believing only after Jesus' death. In many ways it is a very human scene. Peter and the others decide to go fishing rather than face the recent tragedy of their Master, but they are challenged to believe in a resurrected Jesus and to witness rather than fish. Peter finds himself restored and challenged to mission.

We have not been invited to breakfast by the sea with the risen Jesus, so how shall we read this? Certainly, it has comforted many who have denied in more ways than one, and yet long to be restored to the faith that saves from perishing. But perhaps this should be read as a wider question from the one whom Paul says "makes intercession for us" (Rom 8:34 KJV): Do I still cast my life on the side of God?

Notes

[1]This is the one place in John's Gospel that uses apocalyptic language. John was concerned with the eschatological, not apocalyptic. He was strongly influenced by eschatological ideas but hardly at all by apocalyptic thought. I believe it is eschatology that has to assume apocalyptic faith. Perhaps his use of apocalyptic language early in his Gospel signals this. His strong affirmation of the victory of light over darkness is, at the very least, subtly apocalyptic, if not overtly so.

[2]Not enough has been made of this brief but important reference to the kindled "faith" or belief of the "other apostle" made purely on the basis of seeing the empty tomb.

[3]I have already noted Paul's use of the passive verb *opthe* ("appeared") in 1 Corinthians 15, which carries with it the connotation to "discern" or to "perceive." The perfect tense of the verb *horao*, "to see," is used here. It occurs twenty times in this Gospel. It carries with it both in classical and *koine* Greek the connotation "to see with the mind." I am indebted to Professor Charles Reed of the faculty at Queens College for pointing out to me that there are a number of passages in both classical Greek philosophy and drama that display this same sense of *horao*, in both the active and passive voices. (See Soph. *Electra*, line 1945 and *ipus ad Colonos*, line 136.) The discussion in Kittel, *Theological Dictionary of the Bible* (Stuttgart, Germany: W. Kohlhammer Verlag, 1970), of John 16:16, "You will see me" notes that "this seeing is neither sensual nor mental perception. It is the encounter with Jesus that takes place in faith under the work of the Holy Spirit. . . . The reference is not merely to sense perception (eyewitness of the story of Jesus) or intellectual perception (consideration of this story), but also to a further seeing, namely, the decision which is taken in encounter with Jesus and which is a turning to faith" (362). The suggestion of "further seeing" leaves room for something that is neither bound to the literal nor the metaphorical. But it does leave much room for an encounter under the power of the Holy Spirit that leads to faith.

CHAPTER 7

THE APOCALYPTIC CHRIST IN REVELATION

We have seen that the witness to the resurrection is often shaped in terms of apocalyptic language and thought by the Gospel writers. The book of Revelation draws even more deeply and directly on the apocalyptic tradition. As such, it gives us vital clues and fresh insight into the meaning of the resurrection, for the exalted Christ stands at the center of the book. His death and resurrection are seen as the decisive events in the battle over evil. For John of Patmos, Rome was the epitome of evil.

Revelation is set in Asia Minor around the years 90–95 CE, some sixty years after the crucifixion of Jesus. John, the presumed author, explains that he is on the island of Patmos "because of the word of God and the testimony of Jesus" (1:9). Soon, if not already, his Christian friends in the churches of Asia Minor will feel the weight of the Emperor Domitian's persecution. Domitian has proclaimed himself "Lord and God" and is to be worshiped. The Christians know only one Lord and God. The faithful will die.

While in exile John writes what is now known as the book of Revelation to his friends. A better title may be the "apocalypse of Jesus Christ." The book is written as an epistle and has an apocalyptic literary style. It bears strong influence from Ezekiel, Daniel, and Zechariah—all of which were known both to Jewish and Gentile Christians, since they shared the Hebrew Scriptures. The basic message of the book is that Rome will not win, but will be destroyed by God's judgment. Christians are encouraged to hold fast to their witness to Jesus as Lord. The Greek word for "witness" is the word from which the English word "martyr" is derived. To be a witness in those days meant being a martyr. John sees Jesus as "the faithful witness" (1:5).

"In the Midst of the Lampstands" (1:13)

The opening chapter of Revelation contains a remarkable picture of the risen Jesus in apocalyptic imagery and offers an excellent preaching opportunity as an introductory sermon for a series.[1] It introduces the readers and hearers to apocalyptic language without the more bizarre imagery that comes later. The picture positions the exalted Christ standing "in the midst of the lampstands," a symbol of the risen Christ standing in the midst of his church. John writes:

> I was in the spirit on the Lord's day, and I heard behind me a loud voice like a trumpet . . . Then I turned to see whose voice it was that spoke to me, and on turning I saw seven golden lampstands, and in the midst of the lampstands I saw one like the Son of Man. (1:10, 12)

John is instructed: "Now write what you have seen" (1:19). The method of gospel writing had already been used by Mark, Matthew, and Luke. Some epistles had also been written. What method of expression would provide the greatest expression of encouragement in the coming persecution? John uses the letter format somewhat, in that the book is written to seven churches in Asia Minor. He does not, however, compose the letter in the way Paul would have written. There is "gospel" in Revelation, but not as Mark wrote. One vehicle of expression presented itself: The apocalyptic method would provide the greatest possible canvas on which to paint his picture.

"Write in a book what you see. . . .and on turning I saw" (1:11,12). John sees as Ezekiel and Daniel saw. How can we think of it? In William Blake's "The Marriage of Heaven and Hell," there is a passage where Blake "dines" with the prophets Ezekiel and Isaiah:

> The prophets Isaiah and Ezekiel dined with me and I asked them how they dared so roundly to assert that God spoke to them; and whether they did not think at the time that they would be misunderstood, & so be the cause of imposition. Isaiah answer'd: "I saw no God, nor heard any, in a finite organical perception; but my senses discover'd the infinite in everything, and I was persuaded, & remained confirm'd, that the voice of honest indignation is the voice of God, I cared not for consequences, and I wrote." Then I asked: "Does a firm persuasion that a thing is so, make it so?" He replied: "All poets believe that it does, & in ages of imagination this firm persuasion removed mountains, but nay are capable of firm persuasion of any thing."

"I heard behind me a loud voice . . . Then I turned to see" (vv. 10, 12). John had never seen the risen Jesus of Easter. Rather, in the spirit of Blake, John's senses "discovered the infinite." He is a witness that the voice of faith can be the voice of God. In the case of John and the other apocalypticists, it is also the voice of "faith-indignation" that evil should ever have the day. For John, that faith came to a focus in his vision of the exalted, triumphant Christ standing in the midst of his church. He is clothed in the robes of an intercessory high priest. White is the symbol of purity and holiness. The feet of burnished bronze symbolize great stability and power. His voice "like the sound of many waters" is the combined voice of all the great prophets of God in the past, now coming together in one mighty stream. He holds the church firmly in his hands. The "sharp, two-edged sword" of truth issues from his mouth. Glory shines from his face "like the sun." This is the one whom John wishes his friends to see standing in the midst of his church and holding his church firmly in his hands. This is the "apocalypse" of the risen Jesus who will be revealed and will speak in the remainder of the book.

"I Was Dead . . . I Am Alive Forever" (1:18)

In the first chapter John sees the exalted Christ in the midst of his church. He speaks reassuringly when John falls at his feet "as though dead." "Do not be afraid; I am the first and the last, and the living one. I was dead, and see, I am alive forever and ever, and I have the keys of Death and Hades" (1:17-18). In many ways this is a key statement about the exalted Christ. This message of reassurance is both within time and beyond time. The phrase "I was dead" refers to a point in time. "I am alive forever" is beyond time. The Jesus of earthly time and existence is now exalted beyond earthly time and existence. He is no longer "among the dead," as Luke's "two men in dazzling clothes" announce (24:5).

The exalted Jesus holds "the keys of Death and Hades," the ultimate enemy. Death and Hades symbolize the dreaded end of humanity. Hades was the Greek equivalent of Sheol, a dark and forbidding place one entered after death. Now Jesus has power over death, or as Paul says, "Death no longer has dominion over him" (Rom 6:9b). A cosmic victory is declared.

This victorious Jesus is seen standing "in the midst of the lampstands," that is, in the midst of his church. "The seven lampstands are the seven churches" (1:20). Seven is the universal number, so Jesus can be seen standing in the midst of the Church Universal. He holds the church securely in his hands. In its battle with evil the church is assured of his presence and power. He is also in the midst of his church as the intercessor, the great High Priest of Hebrews 4:14-16, and the one whom Paul sees interceding for us (Rom 8:34). John of Patmos sees the Jesus of the Gospels exalted by God. The Jesus who came preaching the good news of the Kingdom is alive forever.

Apocalyptic faith expresses confidence both in the present and at the end. It sees a present and a future victory over evil. Daniel 12:2 affirms both the triumph of God's people over their enemies and looks for the resurrection of the just to participate in that triumph. John expresses this faith in terms of the exalted Jesus, the apocalyptic Christ. Rome still stands, but carries the seeds of ultimate destruction. The martyrs will be raised to the throne of God. Both in time and beyond time, the victory over evil is proclaimed. The apocalyptic Christ stands both within time and beyond time. The author of 1 John puts it this way: "Beloved, we are God's children now; what we will be has not yet been revealed" (3:2).

Faith in the resurrection of Jesus is here seen as far more than believing that we will live forever. This is to neglect the greatest part of its meaning. Life is only despair and eventual darkness, unless the dualism of good versus evil is broken. It is broken in this faith: "Do not be afraid; I am the first and the last . . . I was dead, and see, I am alive forever." This is the faith that saves, no matter the present face of evil. From the first word that had gone out from Jerusalem, John of Patmos and others had come to this faith that saves and casts out fear. At the feet of this exalted and interceding Christ, the church has listened to both the encouraging and rebuking words in the letters to the seven churches.[2]

"In Heaven Stood a Throne" (4:2)

Apocalyptic faith sees the throne. Ezekiel and Daniel saw it. John of Patmos also sees the throne. Chapter 4 is John's vision of the sovereign Creator upon the throne. Around the throne are "four living creatures," symbolizing all creation; and "twenty-four elders," clothed in white garments and wearing golden crowns on their heads—symbols of the redeemed of all ages. The one seated on the throne is not seen, except in appearance "like jasper and carnelian," the white and red stones of holiness and judgment. In typical apocalyptic effect there are "flashes of lightning and rumblings and peals of thunder" and a "sea of glass" before the throne. In *The Wizard of Oz*, Dorothy finally comes face to face with the Wizard, only to discover that he is a helpless old man, concealing himself behind the scenes and using smoke and mirrors to fool the believer. Here in the poetry of apocalyptic imagery, John looks at the true Sovereignty.

"A Lamb Standing" (5:6)

Chapters 4 and 5 should be understood together. The theme of chapter 4 is the sovereignty of God the creator. Chapter 5 carries the theme of the love of God the Redeemer. John sees "between the throne and the four living creatures and among the elders a Lamb standing as if it had been slaughtered" (5:6). I like the King James phrase, "a Lamb in the midst of the throne." The slain and exalted Lamb, symbolizing the love of God, is also on the Throne. Sovereignty and mercy dwell together. The scroll of the world's history is opened by the Lamb, for he alone is "worthy . . . to receive power and wealth and wisdom and might and honor and glory and blessing" (5:12). The exalted Christ is seen "in the midst of the throne," and the sovereign power and mercy of God reigns over all, both now and at the end. The voices of the redeemed of all ages, all creation, and myriads of angels join in praise "to the one seated on the throne and to the Lamb" (5:13).

"And God Will Wipe Away Every Tear" (7:17)

All the visions in Revelation carry essentially the same theme, but with variations. The theme in chapter 7 is the triumph of God over evil, which John sees epitomized in Rome. But the war continues. Jesus may be exalted now, but evil still comes, seemingly stronger than ever, often resulting in martyrdom.

In the first major vision of his book, chapters 6–7, John sees war, famine, and pestilence riding as the dreaded horsemen of the apocalypse. There are four horses, a rider on a white horse, a red horse, a black horse, and a pale horse. Red, black, and pale symbolize war, famine, and pestilence or death. Some students of Revelation insist the rider symbolizes invasion. There is another, and I believe stronger, interpretation. The rider on the white horse is the exalted Christ, and the cause of Christ is riding against war, famine, and pestilence. John sees their eventual defeat. In the meantime, he sees the martyrs safe in heaven (6:9-11) and the eventual judgment and destruction of evil (6:12-17).

The conclusion of this vision is chapter 7, often read at Christian funerals. The redeemed of all ages are seen in heaven, including the martyrs who have come "out of the great ordeal" (7:14). There follows a poem or hymn, perhaps an early Christian hymn, that ends with the picture of God wiping away "every tear from their eyes."

"Now" and "Then"
(6:10)

Because of the concept of time and the continuation of evil, it is difficult to understand the exalted and victorious Christ. God has the victory "then," but also "now"—the now of the martyrs, the now of evil, the now that all of us know when wrong seems forever on the throne and there is no ease for those who try be faithful. The martyrs safe in heaven ask: "Sovereign Lord, holy and true, how long will it be before you judge and avenge our blood on the inhabitants of the earth?" (6:10). There is no answer, except they were given a white robe and told to "rest a little longer, until the number would be complete both of their fellow servants and of their brothers and sisters, who were soon to be killed" (6:11).

"I Saw . . . a White Horse" (19:11)

> Then I saw heaven opened, and there was a white horse! Its rider is called Faithful and True, and in righteousness he judges and makes war. His eyes are like a flame of fire, and on his on his head are many diadems; . . . He is clothed in a robe dipped in blood, . . . And the armies of heaven . . . following him on white horses. From his mouth comes a sharp sword with which to strike down the nations, . . . On his robe and on his thigh he has a name inscribed, "King of kings and Lord of lords." (19:11-16).

After acknowledging the anguish of waiting, John draws this magnificent picture that defines in splendid apocalyptic language the triumph of heaven, which is both now and then. John looks upward to the rider on the white horse followed by the armies of heaven. There is no greater picture of the exalted Christ than this: "He is clothed in a robe dipped in blood . . . and on his thigh he has a name inscribed, "King of kings and Lord of lords." John understands that the centerpiece of Christian faith is the exalted Christ whom he sees here in rich apocalyptic symbolism. John's vision of the risen Christ standing in the midst of his church and riding in triumph, followed by the armies of heaven, requires nothing less than the breadth and depth of an apocalyptic canvas to encompass its dimensions.

John, as a true apocalypticist, sees God's victory brought about by the rider on the white horse. He "judges and makes war" with the weapons of "righteousness." His sword is the sharp two-edged sword of truth, and he is called Faithful and True. By the weapon of truth he smites and rules the "nations." God has highly exalted him. John declares him "King of kings and Lord of lords." The risen Jesus is God's word that righteousness and truth win. All else goes down to destruction.

"See, I Am Making All Things New" (21:5)

In Revelation 20-22 John draws a great picture of hope in rich apocalyptic imagery. The crucified and risen Christ has bound the dragon, or the power of evil, and assured its destruction (20:2). The decisive battle has been fought and won at the cross, followed by the exaltation of Jesus. In the meantime, followers may become martyrs, and the church on earth is still the church militant. The church now lives between the times, between the decisive battle won and the end. But John sees the end. Evil is destroyed forever in a "lake of fire" (20:10). The throne becomes one of judgment. The scales are balanced. "He shall come to judge the quick and the dead," as the Apostles' Creed says.

The sovereign throne is beyond time, as are the "new heaven" and "new earth" (21:1). He hears a voice from the Throne: "See, the home of God is among mortals. He will dwell with them as their God; . . . he will wipe away every tear from their eyes. . . . And the one who was seated on the throne said, 'See, I am making all things new' " (21:3, 4, 5). We are in "now" and beyond "now." Witness the fact that Christians continue to read these and other comforting words in this chapter, when they commit loved ones to God. For those of faith, this is always "now." Now God makes "all things new." Now God "wipes away every tear." Now the Holy City comes down from God. Now are the gates of pearl and the streets of gold. And it will also be "then" at the "end"—whenever that will be. The victory of God is declared. When all else has fled away, the throne remains, and the "Lamb in the midst of the throne." What was done at the cross by the power of suffering, love conquers.

Here John's voice blends with the voices of Ezekiel and Daniel. There is Ezekiel's assurance to Israel in exile: "I am going to open your graves, and bring you up from your graves" (37:12). Daniel sees God's people receiving the kingdom and possessing the kingdom "forever and ever" (Dan 7:18). For John and the early Christians, the raising of Jesus is the continuing promise to the faithful that God has triumphed now and will continue to triumph. John is standing with one foot in time—Roman time, martyr time—but with another foot beyond time and even above time. He can see Rome defeated. He can see the martyrs safe in heaven, while looking forward to the end with confidence.

At the End—What?

In view of this, the resurrection faith John is expressing in apocalyptic language is something greater than an exit from a tomb. It is faith in a righteous Creator. The apocalyptic Christ is "passed through the heavens" (Heb 4:14). He is priest and intercessor in the midst of his church. He is the rider on the white horse who judges and makes war. He is at once victory and the promise of victory.

It is said that ancient Israel traveled in the wilderness by a flame of fire by night and a pillar of cloud by day. When apocalyptic faith with its powerful metaphors and symbols is freed from literal chains, it, too, becomes a flame of fire by night and a pillar of cloud by day. It provided power and guidance for John and the early believers. They could believe in the victory at the end, even if indefinitely delayed. Apocalyptic faith can provide power for the believer at any time. The power of John's apocalyptic image of the risen Christ and the "Lamb in the midst of the throne" has not yet been measured.

I have suggested all along that the issue is God's faithfulness. Along with that is the issue of God's sovereignty. Is God able or not? Is there a throne? True and effective faith yields to the sovereignty and mercy of God and the love that raised Jesus from the dead. There is the fiery red carnelian stone of judgment in the throne, but there is also a rainbow around the throne (4:3; see Gen 9:16).

Faith in John's apocalypse is called to "wait . . . . until"—"until the number would be complete both of their fellow servants and of their brothers and sisters, who were soon to be killed" (6:11). Wait! Wait? The war has not ended. Wait in faith "until." This is part of what Joseph Sittler called "the anguish of preaching." It is also part of the anguish of believing. I do not see how preaching or personal faith can avoid that anguish or keep it away by bright and cheerful looks and some advice on positive thinking. Not that the preacher should be gloomy, but that the preacher and all of us should be honest. Preaching the apocalyptic Christ is preaching that word "until" and the Jesus of earth whom Matthew says cried "My God, why . . . ?" (Matt 27:46)

Believing in the victory of the apocalyptic Christ is believing that righteousness and truth win. This means that faith choices must be made, for sooner or later what is untrue and unrighteous emerges, and evil bears within it the seeds of its own ultimate destruction. "God will wipe away every tear (7:17) and make "all things new" (21:5).

It is unfortunate that the book of Revelation has been made a subject of so much controversy concerning the "end." We finite human beings cannot understand infinity; and the only terms we have to talk about infinity are finite terms. This means that we should put our hands over our mouths before we rush to take a position on that which is beyond our ken. But it does not mean that we cannot look "beyond" in faith, using whatever poor finite terms we have, as John does when he talks about heaven in terms of "gates of pearl" and "streets of gold." We can walk this earth and think of heaven. We can look up and see the rider on the white horse clothed in a robe dipped in blood and followed by the armies of heaven. Apocalyptic faith does not call us to paint dark and gloomy pictures of the end. It calls us to believe that at the end the victorious love of God will be there, and "death will be no more" (21:4).

Notes

[1]I have found that teaching Revelation in a series of informal sessions is a better way to prepare for preaching from Revelation. This is not to say that there are not great preaching opportunities in the book. The seven letters, of course, present preaching opportunities, but I hope they would be used with sympathy and not simply to chastise the church! In general, however, there must first be an understanding of what apocalyptic writing is and is not.

[2]My book *The Dragon Bound* (Atlanta: John Knox Press, 1981) ch. 2, has a further exposition of the book of Revelation and how it speaks to our time, and particularly to the church through the messages to the seven churches.

CHAPTER 8

BELIEVING AND PREACHING THE REVELATION OF JESUS

Throughout this book I have made suggestions for "believing and preaching," but have not given sermons. I hope I have given preachers some helpful insight toward sermon preparation. I can think of many books that have helped me preach without giving the full sermon from a text or passage. Since I believe preaching is truth delivered through personality, preaching the truth of the resurrection should be delivered by each individual preacher through his or her own unique personality.

Faith is always at stake when the resurrection is the question. I have written for the preacher and hearer who have difficulty with a literal view of the resurrection appearances, but who still believe God has raised and exalted Jesus. Certainly, if the faith of the preacher is at stake, so is the faith of the hearer.

If the hearer comes to the sermon with the expectation that "a word from the Lord" will be heard, the preacher comes with the necessity of speaking that word. Both expectation and necessity join to produce the relevancy of the sermon. In the speaking and in the hearing something happens. In the case of the resurrection of Jesus, what expectation does the hearer bring? If the hearer expects to be convinced beyond a shadow of a doubt, this is placing too great a burden on the sermon.

The preacher should be relieved of this responsibility immediately, both by the hearer and by the preacher. Also, if the hearer expects to hear that he or she is going to live forever, that may be asking less than the sermon should say. If the preacher feels the need to prove the resurrection, too great a burden is placed upon the preacher and the sermon, and the hearer may rightfully say that this sounds too confident to be true.

The New Testament makes no claim to compel faith beyond a shadow of a doubt. The New Testament is concerned with affirming something about God and asking for a commitment of faith. When we preach the resurrection or hear it preached, a question about God should be considered first and last: Can God be trusted? Always between the cross and the empty tomb there is the cry of dereliction: "My God, my God, why have you forsaken me?" (Matt 27:46). The preacher must hear that cry before any sermon is attempted on the resurrection, for that cry may be echoed from the pews.

Seeing Angels Before Tombs

Doubt should be allowed in church, not that we are to preach our doubts; we are to preach our faith. But the preacher and the hearer must come together in the Easter proclamation and hear unflinchingly the cry of Jesus from the cross. The preacher hears that cry in his or her work as a pastor and within himself or herself as a human being. The person in the pew hears, but wonders if it is right to bring it into church. Whether it is right or not, we do bring it into church. So I would ask both preacher and hearer: Why not bring doubt first to the empty tomb? After all, according to the Gospels, this is what the first believers did. They thought Jesus was "among the dead." Their hopes were gone and possibly their faith. Why not begin Easter by first coming along with the first community of faith? I believe it is not only right but necessary for the sermon to give evidence that the preacher understands this feeling and may indeed share it.

With that honesty, glibness has already left by the side door. Flowering over everything with Easter lilies loses its sheen. Instead, we are walking with Mary Magdalene and the other women to pay our last respects. We are looking with Peter and "the other disciple" into an empty tomb. There are no hallelujah choruses heard on that walk. The only thing on our minds is the stone before the tomb, perhaps the stone in our own hearts. The preacher and the hearer join hands, for they are walking the same walk.

I once heard of an Easter service where the people entered the church and found it dark and bare, with no appointments for worship visible—no cross, no Bible, no paraments at the lectern and pulpit. The organ was silent. The silence was great, but something was heard in that silence—the darkness. Then someone entered and read the last verses of Mark's Gospel. The tomb was declared empty, and the "young man dressed in a white robe" made his announcement again: "He has been raised. He is not here." Then the lights came up. There were the sounds of a drum and the organ. The young people of the church carried in paraments, banners, a Bible, and a cross. The people rose to sing in faith: "Christ the Lord is risen today." Angels might have been seen outside tombs.

Revelatory Moments

Apocalyptic images, colors, and sounds, including angels, should be seen and heard for what they are—a great call to faith without certainty. The poet will tell me that the sunset is beautiful and that I am to find strength in the beauty, but I must do so knowing that the sun rises and sets upon the pain and darkness of the world. Apocalyptic imagery and language do the same. They call for faithfulness and trust in God, despite all the evidence to the contrary.

Paul affirmed this faith in the face of darkness: "We are accounted as sheep to be slaughtered" (8:36). He recites a catalog of terrors: "hardship, distress, persecution, famine, nakedness, peril, sword." But out of that darkness comes the affirmation of faith: Nothing "will be able to separate us from the love of God in Christ Jesus our Lord" (8:35, 39). The cry of dereliction between the cross and the empty tomb is not canceled. Rather, it is overlaid by the faith that God has not forsaken. Can the preaching and the hearing rise above the "Why"? Can we preach and hear that "we are accounted as sheep to slaughtered" while also affirming that nothing can "separate us from the love of God"? Both must be preached, if honesty is to be found in the sermon; and both must be held, if honesty is to be found in the faith.

There are those who have difficulty seeing angels before tombs. I have often found a wistfulness among those who cannot see angels sitting before tombs. I can still hear the person quietly asking out of the blue, "Can I believe?" Before replying with some creedal word, I needed to hear "Can I believe?" The preacher needs to hear that question before composing a sermon. The hearer needs to know that she can ask the question. Behind "Can I believe?" is the question "Can I hope and trust in God, even if I cannot visualize literally what happened at the tomb or in the upper room?" More importantly, "Can I hope and trust in God in the face of my own darkness?"

Out of this honest walk to the tomb and out of the gatherings in the upper rooms of fear can come revelatory moments. They can happen in sermons when the preacher and hearer join hands on the way to the burial place or sit together in some upper room of fear, or when some Mary Magdalene makes her way to the tomb.

In the National Gallery in London, there is a remarkable painting by Savolde called *St. Mary Magdalene Approaches the Tomb*. The artist portrays Mary hesitantly approaching the tomb and captures a look of the first dawning hope upon her face and in her eyes. There is both a question and perhaps the beginning of a gleam of surprise. But above all there is a look that asks: "What does this mean?" It is a revelatory moment.

There are no angels in the picture. Everything is in the look in Mary's eyes, which carries with it even a hint of laughter.

With both hesitancy and hope, the preacher and hearer approach the tomb together. Preaching and hearing the resurrection are done best at the edge of hope, at the edge of darkness, where the light is always forced to live. The moments hanging between hope and despair can be great moments of revelation. I prefer not to spell out those moments in precise detail. But when they happen, angels roll away stones, and Christ's shalom is heard behind doors of fear.

Seeing the Throne

When the resurrection is preached and heard, the preacher and hearer should see the throne. In other words, they should believe in a sovereign God. By sovereign I refer to Mark's terminology: "The kingdom (Rule) of God has come near; repent (turn) and believe in the good news" (1:15). The word "sovereign" needs to be retranslated into today's language, and that retranslation begins with the old affirmation that God is in control. It asks us to turn (repent) from looking at the darkness and to believe this, the best of news. Unless this was believed in Ezekiel's day, the promise of the restoration of Israel was an empty promise. It was not the "wheel" that Ezekiel saw "way up in the middle of the air" that gave him hope. It was the sovereignty that the wheel symbolized. It was that same throne John of Patmos saw that gave him hope that Rome would not prevail (Rev 4).

It may be the most difficult part of preaching and believing, especially when the victory of the good seems a vain hope. Before affirming this sovereignty, and certainly before attempting to retranslate it, the preacher is called to sit with Ezekiel and the exiles. The preacher will have been with Isaiah in the Temple when Uzziah dies or with John on Patmos when the martyrs die. The resurrection and the sovereignty of God are preached with these ideas in the forefront. The sovereignty of

God is thrust against anything else that claims sovereignty. It is a bold stand that faith takes, to challenge anything else that claims the sovereignty—this present pain, or guilt, the current evil that rides roughshod over human rights and destroys peace. But preaching and believing the resurrection of Jesus do precisely that. Repent and believe the good news that God rules and that the love and judgment of God is sovereign. The turn is the beginning of the faith choice. The turn is the beginning of salvation and the defeat of the evil that threatens our souls.

"There will be more joy in heaven over one sinner who repents," declared Jesus (Luke 15:7), as he told the stories of the lost sheep, the lost coin, and the lost son. We can be lost in many ways. We can be afraid, lonely, under pressure, or worried to death about something we cannot share with anyone else. We can be lost in a childhood trauma. We can be lost with too much money or not enough money. We can be lost in our hopes, fears, and guilt. We can be lost in the busy, demanding, and even exciting world, so that we wake up one Wednesday afternoon to discover we have lost a sense of God. And with it all, we can be lost when we try to live outside the sovereignty of God, living without seeing the throne. It is from this that we are called to "turn." When the turning happens, there is the sound of apocalyptic angels who are charged always to announce the victory of God.

Earlier I referred to a friend who likes to think of the resurrection faith experience as like falling in love. You cannot describe the experience, but it is wonderful! So it is with the faith choice of turning toward the good news that God rules and Jesus has not been allowed to fall to the ground. Crying "repentance" need not mean wearing sackcloth and ashes. It can be presented and heard as a turning toward light and joy, the shalom-peace that Jesus gave in the upper room, and the voice of the Shepherd who seeks the lost. It can be presented and heard with angels declaring the victory of light over darkness. Mary Magdalene (or her present-day counterpart) can leave the empty tomb, declaring, "I have seen the Lord."

Two Angels

There are two angels who are most prominent in the story of the resurrection of Jesus. The first angel is the Christmas angel who announced "good news of a great joy" (Luke 2:10). The other angel sat upon the stone before the empty tomb in Matthew's Gospel (28:2). Christmas faith needs to see the angel on the stone. Easter faith needs the voice of the Christmas angel. The act of God in sending Jesus is "good news of a great joy." But that joy is complete when the Easter angel announces "He is risen." The "good news of a great joy" is the faithfulness of a loving and sovereign Creator, whose love is for all creatures great and small. Grace is greater than evil, and forgiveness is possible. The darkness that tears at the human soul does not have the final word. A healing word is spoken to the mystery of human pain: The Jesus who bore the pain is the exalted Son of God, who "intercedes for us" (Rom 8:34). This is good news for everyone and condemns no one (John 3:16-17). This good news is intended for "all the people" (Luke 2:10). Not one sparrow falls to the ground (Matt 10:29) without God's knowledge.

Then Comes the End

Apocalyptic faith declares that God will win in the end. Ezekiel raises this faith, when comforting the exiles in Babylon. John of Patmos does the same for Christians in Asia Minor. When the resurrection of Jesus is understood in this light, it becomes a powerful affirmation that embraces more than the lilies of Easter Sunday. If life, the world, and time have their beginning with God, then the resurrection has its end with God. The kingdom-rule of God is over all life, the world, and time. For this reason Jesus taught his disciples to pray: "Your kingdom come. Your will be done, on earth as it is in heaven" (Matt 6:10).

Jesus did not dwell on the "end." He was content with affirming God's victory at the end and talked about peace-making, love, justice, mercy, and other things that make life good and compassionate. Paul expected the end in his lifetime, but that did not seem to get in the way of his calling for a life of "faith, hope, and love" or of the duty of loving one's neighbor as oneself. John of Patmos may have expected Rome to collapse before his eyes, but that did not prevent him from calling for faithfulness and righteousness to the end—whenever that might be. But calendars get in the way, as Christians declare themselves to be of one view or another as to what will happen at the end. All the while the faith concerning the end begs to be addressed, and its call to faithfulness expressed. This certainly means a call to ethics, doing justice, loving mercy, and walking humbly with God (Mic 6:8). Before the end, there is still the matter of what is right and what is wrong.

As to the end, will it be "now" or "then"? Does it really matter? The present always seems to be fading quickly into the past. The years of God's created time continue, while the angelic announcement remains: "He is risen." This word continues to shine in the darkness, and the darkness has not been overcome. The first communities of faith found their courage in this faith, which continues to create and sustain new communities, "until that day" (2 Tim 1:12).

Apocalyptic Messengers

This is a special word to my colleagues in the ministry of preaching: Those who represent this faith become, in effect, apocalyptic messengers. A pastor friend was telling me of a visit to a parishioner who had been stricken with a very serious illness. The man said he appreciated the visit very much and was greatly helped. My friend wondered what he had said. I suggested that he had been an "apocalyptic messenger" by his presence and assurance of hope in God. The apocalyptic message of hope in God is for the person suffering an overwhelming illness, or to those who look out upon a world struggling with good and evil. The darkness may be terrifying, but it has been overcome: "He is not here. He is risen." To be sure, this does not take away the illness, nor does it bring instant peace and good will to the world. It does, however, cast one's life on the side of "light" and gives meaning to the struggle. Indeed, it urges on the struggle. It can look forward to the end, believing that the love of God is here "now" and will be there "then." It always summons light against the dark.

What other faith is strong enough to challenge despair and cynicism and to summon light against the dark? The apocalyptic faith born in despair can be heard with power whenever it is placed against cynicism and despair. In apocalyptic language, the dragon of Revelation does not win, for the rider on the white horse is followed by the armies of heaven (Rev 19). The apocalyptic Christ still lives in the midst of his church. Whoever presents this message is an apocalyptic "angel" of comfort and hope in the spirit of Ezekiel who announced in the name of the Lord: "I am going to open your graves, and bring you up from your graves . . . and I will bring you back" (37:12).

The Faith That Becomes Hope and Mission

In our time we read and hear much about the decline of the church. I place these analyses against the first communities of faith, remembering the remarkable burst of evangelical energy that came from them. The faith that God has exalted Jesus becomes both hope and mission. Even though the early Christians tried to stay in Jerusalem, they could not. The power of their faith had to break out in Paul, for example, or in the person who wrote Hebrews 11, or in John of Patmos, or in the Gospel writers. That power can and does still break out. There is one still "in the midst of the lampstands" (Rev 1:13).

Mission is resident in this faith. What fight for justice and human rights does it require? Churches that emphasize only "saving souls" seem to thrive and grow ever larger while they have a monopoly on having a mission and being "evangelical." Of course, souls are to be saved, but evil also is to be challenged wherever it is found. It is nowhere suggested that we are to wait for the end and allow God to do all the work. The challenge against evil and the stand for justice are part of the perpetual mission of the church. The softening of that challenge blurs and softens mission. Gaining numbers at the expense of mission will gain nothing.

Of course, this faith is the beginning of the soul's salvation, the lighting of the candle of hope that the darkness cannot overcome. What happened in the Jerusalem upper room is important, but also important is what happens in my "upper room." What doors are shut upon what fear? What is it on the other side that grimaces and gestures obscenely, declaring that it has the victory? The witness from the empty tomb is that the exalted Christ appears on the other side of all those shut doors and brings his peace.

Does this faith have to come with supreme and immediate certainty? Perhaps. But this faith may have to live trembling in some upper room of fear. It may have to live long at the edge of doubt and fear that will not go away. Better that it live trembling, than it not live at all. As for the church today, trembling before the analyses of its demise, let it recover the vision of the exalted Christ "in the midst of the lampstands," holding his church in his hands. Let it be believed and preached, even when good is nailed to a cross, the ovens are hot in concentration camps, wrong seems "forever on the throne," and one's own personal evil holds sway.

Let angels dance upon stones! This is what the Gospel writers, Paul, and John of Patmos do for us. Their language becomes apocalyptic color and sound. They paint upon a large canvass when they turn to the matter of the empty tomb and the revelatory experiences with the exalted Christ. Only apocalyptic language will do when we talk of the cosmic work of God in Christ. So let there be earthquakes. Let rocks be split. Let angels roll away stones before an empty tomb and dance for joy.